Migration and Underdevelopment

Westview Special Studies
in Social, Political, and Economic Development

Gordon Donald, *Credit for Small Farmers in Developing Countries*

John S. Gilmore and Mary K. Duff, *Boom Town Growth Management: A Case Study of Rock Springs—Green River, Wyoming*

Donald R. Mickelwait, Mary Ann Riegelman and Charles F. Sweet, *Women in Rural Development: A Survey of the Roles of Women in Ghana, Lesotho, Kenya, Nigeria, Bolivia, Paraguay and Peru*

Elliott R. Morss, John K. Hatch, Donald R. Mickelwait and Charles F. Sweet, *Strategies for Small Farmer Development: An Empirical Study of Rural Development Projects in Gambia, Ghana, Kenya, Lesotho, Nigeria, Bolivia, Colombia, Mexico, Paraguay and Peru*

Paul Shankman, *Migration and Underdevelopment: The Case of Western Samoa*

While many studies of migration focus on urbanization, ethnicity, and psychological adaptation, this book is concerned with the kinds of economic ties that migrants maintain with those left behind. Remittances and their impact on labor-exporting areas are given special attention. Following a review of the literature on the relationship between migration, remittances and underdevelopment, a case study of Western Samoa is presented. Since over one-half of the personal income in Western Samoa derives from remittances, it is possible to examine the economic, political and social effects of remittance dependence and to focus especially on the decline of agricultural production and the increase in import consumption. The study includes Samoan data from both national and village levels. It concludes with a discussion of remittance dependence in other Pacific Islands, with a discussion of similar processes throughout underdeveloped areas of the world, as well as a consideration of the relationship between migration and cultural conservatism.

Paul Shankman received his Ph.D. from Harvard University. He conducted fieldwork in Western Samoa in 1969-1970 and briefly in 1966 and 1973. Some of his publications have appeared in *American Anthropologist* and *Natural History Magazine*. He currently teaches in the Department of Anthropology at the University of Colorado, Boulder.

Paul Shankman

Migration and Underdevelopment

The Case of Western Samoa

Westview Press
Boulder, Colorado

Copyright 1976 by Westview Press, Inc.

Published 1976 in the United States of America by

Westview Press, Inc.
1898 Flatiron Court
Boulder, Colorado 80301
Frederick A. Praeger, Publisher and Editorial Director

Library of Congress Cataloging in Publication Data

Shankman, Paul
  Migration and underdevelopment.

  Bibliography: p. 113
  1. Emigrant remittances—Western Samoa. 2. Western
Samoa—Emigration and immigration. 3. Western Samoa
—Economic conditions. I. Title.
HG3998.W4S47   330.9'96'14   75-38692
ISBN 0-89158-022-0

Printed and bound in the United States of America.

Contents

List of Tables

Acknowledgements

This small volume owes a great deal to a number of
people and institutions. Research was made possible
by a National Institute of Mental Health Fellowship
#1-F0l-MH 46152-01 and Field Training Grant, by a
National Science Foundation Summer Training Grant,
and by a grant from the University of Colorado Council
on Research and Creative Work. Among the individuals
who deserve special thanks are: Mrs. P.J. Epling and
the late Dr. P.J. Epling without whose encouragement
this study would not have been possible; Dr. John W.M.
Whiting, whose patience and guidance were extremely
valuable; and Klaus-Friedrich Koch and Waldemar R.
Smith, whose sound advice was followed. In Western
Samoa, my Samoan family, friends, and the people of
the village of Sa'asi (a pseudonym) were all very
generous with their time and hospitality. In the Post
Office Department, the cooperation of Mr. E. Betham,
Mr. E. Williams, and Mr. M. Efaraimo was very helpful.
During the preparation of the manuscript, Barbara
Ellington provided invaluable research assistance,
while my wife Sally edited its many versions. Terry
James performed the thankless task of typing the
manuscript and coped with its endless revisions.
Finally, the governments of Western Samoa and Tonga
deserve a note of appreciation for allowing still
another anthropologist to investigate their countries.
Needless to say, responsibility for errors of fact and
interpretation rest with the author.

MAP OF THE SOUTHWEST PACIFIC
WITH WESTERN SAMOA AND
AMERICAN SAMOA

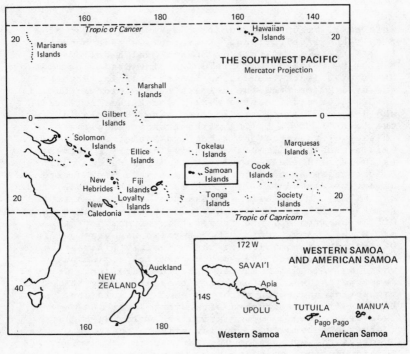

Introduction

THE SETTING AND THE PROBLEM

Underdevelopment is a harsh word, and Samoa must seem an
improbable spot for an inquiry into the realities of
economic vulnerability in the contemporary world. Not
so long ago, the islands were regarded as the very
antithesis of underdevelopment. At that time, the
physical beauty of the islands was equated with the
mystique of a tropical paradise and even today a certain
romantic imagery persists. Perhaps because this imagery
has been so effectively conveyed in the works of Margaret
Mead, Somerset Maugham, and Robert Louis Stevenson, there
remains a temptation to think of Samoa as still another
Polynesian idyll bound by the rhythms of indigenous life.
Yet if this idyll ever existed, it has long since vanished,
while the very real problems of underdevelopment have
become apparent.

The islands have not been isolated from contemporary
affairs. For over a century, Samoa has been the object
of international rivalries and deliberations. In 1889,
great-power colonial disputes nearly erupted into a major
naval confrontation between Germany, Great Britain, and
the United States just off the coast of the islands.
This conflict was avoided only after a violent storm
scuttled some of the warships. Later, at the turn of
the twentieth century, a territorial division of the
islands peacefully resolved the hostilities with the
United States acquiring what was to become American
Samoa, while the large islands of Upolu and Savai'i
became Western Samoa. Western Samoa was administered
by the Germans until World War I, when the islands fell
under New Zealand mandate. Discontent with the New
Zealand administration, however, led to a small-scale

revolt by Samoans, sowing the seeds of nationalism.
Finally, in 1962, these nationalist aspirations were
realized with the founding of Western Samoa, the country
with which this study is concerned.

During the colonial period, the people of Western Samoa
became part of a state-level polity and an agricultural
export economy. The indigenous political system adjusted
to the exigencies of centralized government while the
economy became oriented toward copra production for the
world market. Today the majority of the people continue
to live in the rural villages that dot the islands'
coastline. Using a variation of the slash-and-burn
technique, they cultivate fragmented plots of land,
growing coconuts, bananas, and taro for their own subsistence as well as for export. Rural villagers comprise
most of Western Samoa's 155,000 citizens, but of this
total about 11% are part-Samoans and Europeans. Unlike
the majority of the population, the part-Samoans and
Europeans live in and around the port town of Apia; it
is this group that controls the agricultural export trade
of the islands and that constitutes the economic elite.

Agriculture has been the basis of the Western Samoan
economy for the past century. Currently, however, the
agricultural situation is changing. The Samoan population
has been rapidly expanding while most of the islands'
agricultural land has already been cleared. Within the
next 15 years, almost all such land will be in use,
putting considerable pressure on an agricultural system
that relies on fallow periods for soil regeneration. In
addition to looming land shortages, Western Samoa's
economy is faced with decreasing agricultural productivity; per capita export production of cash crops has
been declining for some time. Furthermore, large
fluctuations in world market prices for copra have
meant that average income from agricultural exports has
hardly risen since World War II. Although people in the
port town do fairly well, the average rural agriculturalist
makes considerably less than $US 100 a year.

Such adverse trends are not encouraging, and since
independence in 1962, the new nation of Western Samoa
has had to contend with these problems of underdevelopment.
Yet the present situation does not seem, on the surface,
to be particularly troublesome. In fact, Western Samoa
is in the midst of a consumer boomlet of sorts. In both
the port town and rural villages, the casual observer is
impressed by the material changes that have occurred

x

since the early 1960s. There are a startling number of
new cars and houses; there is a diversity of consumer
goods; the personal appearance of most Samoans has been
conservative, but in 1973, long hair, sideburns, mustaches,
and even beards were commonplace. Young Samoans were
becoming "teenagers" complete with T-shirts emblazoned
with "hippie" and "peace." Mini-skirts and bell-bottom
pants were very much in vogue in the port town. The
radio station played the latest in rock and easy-listening
music, as well as some "oldies but goodies," and while
there is a certain amount of irony involved in listening
to "It Never Rains in Southern California" in the middle
of Western Samoa, Samoans like the new sound. They also
have definite taste preferences. In 1970, Rothman's
cigarettes and Steinlager beer were very popular, but
in 1973, Marlboros and Leopard beer were in demand.
Samoans want what Europeans have, and their fundamental
problem is how to meet these wants in a *deteriorating*
economy.

While Samoans have increased their consumption of imported
goods, agricultural production continues to decline.
This paradoxical trend of consuming more while producing
less is, in large part, the result of migration and remittances. The decline of agriculture has helped to
stimulate migration abroad, particularly to New Zealand.
Remittances--sums of money sent or brought back by the
migrants--have made it possible for Samoans to increase
import consumption. Yet while remittances contribute to
the look of modernity on an individual and family level,
they also create major balance of payments problems, contributing to underdevelopment at the national level.

Although migration and remittances presently play an
important role in the Western Samoan economy, fifteen
years ago they were of only marginal significance.
Since then, remittances have moved from a minor, supplementary source of income for islands to a position
so vital that migrant remittances are the chief source
of personal income for Western Samoans. In 1974, remittances comprised more than one-half of the islanders'
personal income, and officials state, without exaggeration,
that "people are our most valuable export."

The problem-focus of this study is the relationship
between migration, remittances, and underdevelopment.
The case material from Western Samoa illuminates this
problem-focus, but Western Samoa is not a unique
case. As we shall see, the islands are a microcosm of
processes occurring throughout underdeveloped areas of

the world. It is therefore necessary to place the data
from Western Samoa in a comparative context in order to
understand its implications. Apart from detailing a
particular case, then, this study may add to a growing
body of literature dealing with migration and remittances
in a systematic way.[1]

ORGANIZATION OF CHAPTERS

The format to be followed moves from general considerations
of theory and cross-national trends to the specific case
of Western Samoa. Chapter 1 deals with alternative approaches to migration, remittances, and underdevelopment,
contrasting conventional anthropological approaches to
the approach taken in this study. Chapter 2 begins with
a comparative survey of remittance-dependent economies
and then attempts to delineate some of the major effects
of migration and remittances on labor-exporting areas in
underdeveloped countries. Chapter 3 discusses the nature
of underdevelopment in Western Samoa and its relevance to
migration and remittances at the national level, while
Chapter 4 presents data on remittance dependence in a
rural Western Samoan village. Chapter 5 summarizes the
material from Western Samoa, comments on differing interpretations of the effects of migration and remittances
in the islands, and reviews of the implications of the
data. An appendix will provide the reader with a discussion of fieldwork and data quality.

---

[1]Examples can be found in Gulliver (1955, 1957);
Manners (1965); Frucht (1966, 1968); Caldwell (1969);
Philpott (1970); Ardener, Ardener, and Warmington
(1960); Dirks (1972); and J.L. Watson (1975).

1 Anthropological Approaches to Migration, Remittances, and Underdevelopment

The central concern of this study is the relationship
between migration, remittances, and underdevelopment,
focusing on the kinds of economic ties that migrants
maintain with the people who are left behind. As such,
it is similar to studies of "emigrant communities" (see
J.L. Watson 1975). Yet despite the familiarity of researchers with migration and remittances, their
significance in underdeveloped areas has sometimes been
overlooked. For example, in the peasant village of
Tzintzuntzan described by anthropologist George Foster,
almost half of the adult males have migrated to the
United States on a temporary basis (1967:29, 286-287).
These migrants have remitted substantial sums of money,
contributing to some far-reaching changes in the village.
The same pattern of migration has also brought dramatic
changes to Tepoztlán, another well-known Mexican peasant
village. With almost half of Tepoztlán's adult males
in the United States for varying intervals, Oscar Lewis
notes the effects of migration and remittances:

> In 1943, Tepoztlán suffered from an acute land
> shortage. Now [1957], because in many cases
> the *braceros* return to the village only to rest
> a few months before setting out for another
> period in the United States, it suffers from a
> shortage of manpower, and many *milpas* go un-
> cultivated. The *braceros* earn more in some
> months in the United States than they could earn
> in almost two years in the village, and many
> have invested their savings in improvements
> for their houses and in land and cattle. Many

1

have brought home portable radios, mechanical
toys, clothing, and cloth--the village now has
four full-time tailors who are kept busy providing tailor-made pants for the villagers.
(1960:98)

Given the striking dependence of these two almost
archetypal peasant villages on migration and remittances, it is surprising that relatively little is
said about these important phenomena.

It may be that some of our present research approaches
shed only partial light on the impact of migration
and remittances on underdeveloped economies. Community
studies such as those of Foster and Lewis may relegate
migrant remitters to a marginal position in the village
economy, while studies of migration *per se* may concentrate on migrants to the extent that the kinds of
economic ties maintained by migrants with their families
receive scant mention. Moreover, urban studies tend to
have their own research emphases: urbanization,
ethnicity, acculturation, networks, and psychological
adaptation. As a result, these approaches have tended
to neglect remittances. While this is not intended to
be a criticism of an important body of work (see Miracle
and Berry 1970; Graves and Graves 1974), it does raise
the question of what kind of approach might incorporate
remittances and their impact as a research focus. One
such approach might draw attention to migration and
remittances and their relationship to underdevelopment.

The study of underdevelopment differs in approach from
most anthropological inquiries. As Adams has commented:

> Clearly most societies that anthropologists
> had been studying were underdeveloped; but
> there was little within the anthropological
> literature that threw any very direct light
> on the nature, causes and processes of that
> condition. Just as the processes of change
> in peasant villages could not be understood
> apart from the larger picture, so the process
> of development was impossible to understand
> from a study of fragments. (1970:4)

Like other investigators, Adams has found that the study
of underdevelopment entails a change in the unit of
analysis examined, the kinds of materials gathered, and
the historical scope encompassed. Specifically, there
are three methodological shifts involved:

2

1. The study of underdevelopment requires
   an examination of the *kind of ties* that
   exist between local, national, and international levels.

2. *Economic* factors require the same explicit
   treatment as social, cultural, and noneconomic factors.

3. The study of underdevelopment requires a
   comparative and *historical* perspective.

Although these methodological shifts may seem rather
obvious, they do represent a departure from the
assumptions underlying the synchronic microanalytic
accounts of social factors in development and underdevelopment that dot the literature of economic
anthropology.

Most anthropological studies of economic change in
underdeveloped areas of the world have relied on a
microanalytic approach that views change from the
bottom up. Microanalysis is "the careful observation
and description of variation within a social structure
amenable to first hand, personal observation" (Nash
1965:3). While this approach has helped to correct
some misconceptions, it can lead to a selective
avoidance of the *sources* of change at the national
and international levels. The anthropological emphasis
on 'tradition' and village studies has sometimes obscured
the importance of colonial practice, government policy,
and world finance in the shaping of economic trends.
A consideration of such factors necessitates a macroanalytic approach that views change from the top down.
Yet to adequately comprehend the causes and consequences of underdevelopment, neither macroanalytic nor
microanalytic approaches are sufficient in themselves;
both should be employed (Manners 1965; Frucht 1966;
1968; Adams 1970; Dalton 1971a; Epstein 1975).

Anthropological studies of economic change have also
tended to stress social, cultural, and noneconomic
factors at the expense of economic factors. At one
time, this may have been necessary, but it is now
evident that the study of values, attitudes, religious
beliefs, and family structures does not preclude the
study of economic factors. Carefully controlled
studies indicate that a preoccupation with social,
cultural, and noneconomic factors may be quite limiting
(Rogers 1969; Caldwell 1969; Hayami and Ruttan 1971).

At its worst, this kind of emphasis may amount to a form
of "sociological protectionism" which denies economic
behavior to peasants while stressing social prerequisites to development (Myint 1969:104). It has now been
shown, however, that "there are no social prerequisites
that must be fulfilled *first* in order that economic
development may take place *afterward*" (Firth in Higgins
1968:264). Furthermore, the sociological emphasis has
led to a "paucity of comparable, hard statistical data
on village-level economies" (Dalton 1971b:9). A more
balanced approach would gather both economic and sociological data in order to better explore the relationship
between the two (Edel 1969; Horowitz 1964:196).

Finally, it is necessary to go beyond the single-case,
synchronic approach that characterizes many anthropological studies. Firth has remarked that anthropologists
have been guilty of "literary embalming," of a "retro-
spective, even nostalgic, point of view concerned more
with what had been lost than with what had changed"
(1963a:80). Barth has noted that the synchronic approach
has led to "descriptions of a social system at two
points in time - or even *one* point in time! - and then
to rely on *extrapolation* between these two states or
from the one state, to indicate the course of change"
(1967a:661). It is no wonder that the results are
couched in idealized abstracted sequences such as under-
development/development, tradition/modernity, or the
various unilinear schemes of acculturation and detri-
balization. These idealized states should not be
conceived of as the beginning and end points of
ahistorical sequences but rather as products of specific
historical processes. Given a historical approach using
comparative materials, investigators are less likely to
view underdevelopment as the primeval condition of traditional society and more likely to inquire into the
processes leading to development, underdevelopment, and
the formation of traditional society (Geertz 1963; West
1966; Gilson 1970; Gulliver 1969).

For the study of migration and remittances in Western
Samoa, these methodological shifts entail an examination
of the Western Samoan national economy, the range and
relative importance of remittances and migration, and
the changing economic relationships between village,
nation, and the wider economy. Since remittances cir-
culate through local, national, and international
channels, it is apparent that their study should attend
to the articulation of these channels. It should also be

4

apparent that the Western Samoan case is comparable to other areas in similar circumstances.

The major difficulty with this approach is that it draws on materials outside the normal province of anthropology. Although the problems of cross-disciplinary research are not new to economic anthropology (Firth 1946; Joy 1967), they nevertheless require the investigator to caution readers in anthropology and economics about the possible liberties taken with their material. Anthropologists will find that the meticulous ethnographic detail often reported in monographs has been pared in order to more clearly delineate the research problem.[2] Yet if economists are relieved by the lack of ethnographic detail, they may not be pleased by the absence of formal economic models. Although these models are available (Tidrick 1966; Steglitz 1969; Todaro 1969), the intent here is not to burden readers with either unnecessary formality or jargon. In attempting to bridge disciplinary boundaries, the investigator is placed in an awkward position somewhat akin to the apocryphal Samoan flying overseas for the first time; a stewardess offered the Samoan a hot towel to wipe his nervous brow, but the Samoan, unfamiliar with airline etiquette, ate the towel. We can do no worse.

---

[2] For those who wish to explore the Samoan literature, ethnographic and otherwise, it is very thorough and of very high quality. A partial bibliography would include: Stanner (1953); Rowe (1930); Keesing (1934); Keesing and Keesing (1956); Calkins (1962); McKay (1957); Grattan (1948); Mead (1930); Epling and Eudey (1963); Epling (1967); Freeman (1964); Watters (1958a, 1958b, 1958c); Nayacakalou (1960); Holmes (1957, 1974); Ala'ilima (1965, 1966); Ember (1964); Mercer and Scott (1958); Fairbairn (1964, 1967, 1970a, 1970b, 1971a); Boyd (1969a, 1969b); Davidson (1967); Hirsh (1958); Pirie (1964); Pirie and Barrett (1962); Barrett (1959); R. Ward (1959); Lockwood (1969, 1971); Panoff (1964); Gilson (1970); Pitt (1970); and Tiffany (1975).

2 Migration and Remittances in Comparative Perspective

In her recent review of migration research, Janet Abu-Lughod (1975) discusses some of the problems raised by current studies of migration. Despite the volume of material, Abu-Lughod feels strongly that present approaches have not led to a better understanding of the general causes and consequences of migration; instead, current research approaches have become more particularistic. She remarks:

> Today's studies frequently err in the direction of straight enthnographies. Each recounts the "peculiar customs" of a unique band of migrants. Often there is little ability to distinguish just what is particularly unique about a given case, what is generic to a set of cases (and indeed what constitutes such a set), and what is, if not universal, at least somewhat usual or common to many types. (1975:201)

To correct these problems, Abu-Lughod suggests that researchers employ a framework sufficiently broad so that other researchers can locate their findings and so that new material can be related to past research. In this chapter, the relationship of migration and remittances to underdevelopment is discussed, and alternative interpretations of the effects of migration and remittances are presented and synthesized.

6

DEPENDENCE ON MIGRATION AND REMITTANCES

Migration and remittances play their most important role
in underdeveloped economies because low-income areas are
the major suppliers of migrant wage labor. Underdevelopment is a characteristic of areas with relatively
low income levels when compared to the developed areas
with which they are associated politically and economically. Per capita income is a convenient, if sometimes
misleading, way of expressing levels of development and
underdevelopment (Hagen 1968:13-15; Higgins 1968:
147-148), although such statistics say nothing about the
economic, political, and social processes that have led
to differential income levels. While our working
definitions of development and underdevelopment do not
include the causes of income trends, processes such as
political and economic incorporation, social dislocation,
and economic concentration are vital to understanding
the relationship between developed and underdeveloped
areas. It is these structural processes that help form
the environments that encourage migration and remittance
dependence.

Historically, wage-labor migration and remittances have
been integral parts of underdeveloped economies during
the colonial and postcolonial periods, being associated
with the rise of plantation agriculture, large-scale
mining, and especially the spread of the industrial
revolution. In the wake of the commercialization of
enterprise, underdeveloped regions in Latin America,
Asia, Africa, the Caribbean, and the Pacific have provided migrant wage labor for the more developed regions.
Anthropologists are well aware of the magnitude of
migration in these often remote areas; it should be
noted, though, that migration first occurs and continues
to occur in those areas closest to the centers of commercialization and industrialization.

In Europe, industrialization has been a continual catalyst
to migration. All of the industrialized Western European
nations rely heavily on internal migration (Beijer 1963),
and many rely even more heavily on foreign migrant labor.
It has been estimated that there are as many as 13 million
temporary migrants in Western Europe (A. Ward 1975:24).
In Great Britain, foreign migrants are 6% of the active
labor force; in France, the figure is 7%-8%; in West
Germany, 10%; and in Switzerland, 30% (see Castles and
Kosack 1972). The entire periphery of this industrialized
area is dependent on migrant labor and remittances; the

dependent countries include Ireland, Spain, Portugal,
Italy, Greece, Yugoslavia, and Turkey as well as some
areas in northern Africa and even the Caribbean. In
the early 1970s, Portugal had fully one third of its
labor force working abroad and remitting hundreds of
millions of dollars a year. Greece's 300,000 migrants
were expected to remit $500 million in 1972. In 1970,
Italy's one million migrants sent or brought back over
a billion dollars. In Turkey, remittances are currently
the major source of foreign exchange.

The dependence of the European periphery on migration
and remittances is mirrored in the relationship of
Mexico and the United States. Mexico provides the
United States with migrants numbering in the millions,
although Mexico itself is sometimes cited as a model of
successful development. In 1968, Mexico had a per capita
income of $547 with substantial expansion in all pro-
duction sectors. This wealth, however, was not
uniformally distributed but rather was concentrated
among the rich; the top 50% of the population received
84.6% of all income (Isbister 1971:44). Among the
masses, the high rate of unemployment and very low
real income encouraged, on an annual basis, about
250,000 impoverished Mexicans to migrate illegally to
the United States (at lowest estimates). Since most of
the migrants, legal and illegal, come from that 50% of
the population receiving only 15.4% of Mexico's income,
and since their remittances run in the millions of
dollars, a substantial portion of poor Mexicans' income
must come from the United States (derived from Samora
1971). Similar income trends can be found in the
American dependency of Puerto Rico.

The extent of dependence on migration and remittances is
evident in other underdeveloped areas of the world. A
survey of the "emigrant communities" of southern China
in 1934-1935 showed that up to 81% of family income came
from overseas remitters (Chen Ta 1940:83); this dependence continues even today in Hong Kong. The entire
Caribbean area is also heavily dependent on migration
and remittances, especially the Barbados, British
Honduras, Jamaica, the Bahamas, Trinidad-Tobago,
Montserrat, St. Vincent, and St. Kitts-Nevis-Anguilla.
As Manners notes:

> The *effects* of the cash inflow from remittances
> will, if they are at all significant, be apparent
> to the community researcher. How else, for
> example, could one account for the survival of

the population of St. John in the U.S. Virgin
Islands? By 1955, when I spent a few months
there, cultivation of any kind had been virtually abandoned...But *all* St. Johnians were
dependent upon cash for their survival, and
almost all cash--with the exception of a few
odd jobs like those at the island's hotels--
derived from wages of family members working
in St. Thomas or the United States. (1965:186)

In some Caribbean communities the flow of people and
remittances is so pervasive and so crucial that Dirks
has stated that there is "very little in terms of social
organization that cannot profitably be viewed as a stra-
tegic response toward facilitating these flows" (1972:9).

Sub-Saharan Africa is another heavily dependent area.
(see Gugler 1968 and Mitchell 1970 for surveys). In
West Africa, it has been estimated that there are more
than a million migrants annually. Internal and external
migration in Ghana, Nigeria, and Upper Volta provide
large sums of money for rural relatives. The situation
in southern and eastern Africa is even more striking.
In South Africa alone there are an estimated 2 million
migrants including almost one million from outside the
country (Hance 1970:159). Acute rural poverty accentuates
the importance of remittances. In Bechuanaland, between
1938 and 1942, remittances provided the single most
important source of income, comprising 46.6% of all
cash income (Schapera 1947:159-161). In the same area
today, Lesotho has the greatest dependency on migration
and remittances of any African nation, and perhaps any
nation in the world; with 60% of its labor force absent
in migratory activities at any one time, Lesotho's remittances in 1966 totaled $10.2 million, while its
exports yielded only $6.1 million (Hance 1970:160-161;
see Wallman 1972). In his survey of African migration,
Hance concludes that without migration and remittances,
Lesotho, Rwanda, Burundi, Malawi, Upper Volta, and
Botswana would be much worse off economically. As it
is, these nations are among the most underdeveloped in
the world.

The extent of dependence on migration and remittances is
all the more remarkable given the low wages of the
migrants, who, nevertheless, are somehow able to save a
significant portion of their income and remit it. A. Ward
cites a study indicating that migrants to Switzerland
saved and remitted 28.3% of their net income (1975:32).

9

Miracle and Berry (1970:97) cite data on Mexican migrants remitting as much as 55% of their income, while in the Cameroons, Ardener *et al.* (1960:181) found that, even under conditions where the migrants are in debt to plantation owners, one-fifth of those migrants surveyed saved at least 25% of their income for remittances; often these people saved so much that they could not afford an adequate diet for themselves. In South Africa, studies have shown that many urban migrants live far below minimum subsistence levels (*Manchester Guardian Weekly*, March 17, 1973, page 1), but they manage to save and remit. Even the street dwellers of Calcutta send money to their relatives in rural Indian villages (Lelyveld 1970:136). This brief survey far from exhausts the material on the extent of dependency, but is is sufficient to indicate that the wage-labor migration, remittance-dependence situation is quite widespread. The question remains: to what extent do migration and remittances promote or retard development in remittance-dependent areas?

ECONOMIC EFFECTS OF MIGRATION AND REMITTANCES

There is little doubt that migration and remittances have a variety of economic, political, and social effects on labor-exporting, remittance-receiving areas, but there is some debate as to exactly what these effects are, especially in the economic sphere. The debate revolves largely around the interpretation of African data, although the general arguments are applicable on a global basis. The reason for this debate stems from the fact that these effects can be viewed in several different ways: long- or short-term impact, social or individual impact, or any combination of these. Investigators looking at different kinds of data come up with different ideas as to what the economic effects of migration and remittances really are. In the literature, at least three widely varying interpretations exist. First of all, there is the view that migration and remittances promote economic development. A second view states that migration and remittances help to maintain the economic *status quo*. Lastly, there is a view that contends that migration and remittances contribute to underdevelopment. Let us consider these views in light of some of the available data on remittance-dependent areas.

The most favorable interpretation of migration and remittances is given by economist Elliot Berg, who

states that "the migrant labor system was historically
a stimulus to economic growth and...represents an optimum
allocation of resources under existing conditions"
(1965:176). He demonstrates that migration has improved
income and living standards for migrants and for their
families who receive remittances, and that it does not
adversely affect agricultural production. Over the
short term, remittances raise income levels and provide
other material benefits for labor-exporting areas.

> The analytic balancing of short-term costs and
> benefits from migration thus points to a con-
> siderable net gain for the village economy,
> for while output in the village declines only
> slightly, the aggregate incomes of village
> residents are swelled by the net earnings of
> the migrants. (1965:172)

Berg's analysis makes a good deal of sense. After all,
if migrants did not improve their economic position,
there would be little reason for migration, and the
favorable aggregate-income effect for remittance-
receiving villages is supported by evidence from a
number of studies. However, while his analysis does
apply to the present-day situation in *some* parts of
Africa, it is quite narrow in the range of economic
conditions it covers, its historical scope, and its
stress on *income* as contrasted with the broader economic
transformations that give income statistics their meaning.

Two examples that Berg cites to support his theory are
the Mossi of Upper Volta and the Ngoni of Tanzania. Yet
a closer look at each of these cases might lead to a
different interpretation. The Mossi did not enter the
labor force voluntarily nor did they benefit economically
from their endeavors. Gorer, who observed labor conditions throughout West Africa in the early 1930s,
reported:

> On several occasions the administration has
> settled large groups of the Mossi in the Ivory
> Coast--sixty thousand have been moved to the
> neighborhood of Yammossoukro, in the middle
> of the forest, this year; but the Negroes
> support the changed climate and dietary con-
> ditions so badly--not to mention hard work on
> inadequate pay--that something like half die the
> first year. Private woodcutters and planters
> can also get permission to go and recruit the
> men they need; the local administrator merely

11

tells the chiefs that so many men are required
and are to be delivered at such a place and
date. The men cannot refuse to go.

When men are working away from their village,
they are meant to be fed and housed. What is
more, they sometimes are, though in more than
one case I have seen the Society for the
Prevention of Cruelty to Animals would have
prosecuted me if I had given a dog the same
quantity and quality of food and shelter.
(1935:121-122)

Skinner's more recent study shows that only after the
Mossi had been monetized did they migrate voluntarily,
for

while the Mossi were initially forced to
migrate for work to earn wages to pay taxes,
they now migrate voluntarily because only by
doing so can they satisfy many of the new
needs they have acquired over the past sixty
years. And unless the Upper Volta makes great
economic strides in the near future [they] will
continue to leave their homes in order to earn
money. (1965:84)

One of the "new needs" to which Skinner refers is the
need for more remittances obtained through migration.
The benefits of remittances occur in this case precisely
because of a *lack* of economic alternatives to migration
and a lack of growth in other parts of the economy.

Gulliver's study of the Ngoni makes a somewhat different
but related point about the effects of migration and
remittances:

1. By labor migration men are able to earn
and bring home money and goods that under
present conditions in Ngoni they are unable,
or feel they are unable, to obtain there.
Thus there has been an immediate effect of
raising or at least maintaining the standard
of living at home; but

2. the recourse to labour migration as a
source of income saps the efforts and will
of the Ngoni to work more diligently in
developing the resources of their own fields
and country. There is therefore a depressing

effect on the general tribal economy, and
this is the most serious disadvantage of the
system. (1955:41-42)

Gulliver also notes the harmful social effects of the
migrant-labor system. Remittances comprise about 20%
of the minimum family income in this case (1955:36).

The Bemba, studied by Richards in 1930-31, provide
another interesting case of rural transformation through
migration and remittances. With 40% to 50% of the Bemba
males away annually, three or four old men might be left
in charge of a community. Village cohesion was not
guaranteed, though, because the remainder of the population might leave to join more stable villages. "In
fact, the dead appearance of villages with a large
percentage of absent men is one of the most striking
features of the countryside" (Richards 1961:405). Since
the Bemba were not cash cropping at the time of their
entry into the wider economy, remittances from wage-labor
migration comprised most of the cash sector of the
village economy, but as more migrants left, the net
effect of migration was not to alleviate rural poverty
but to reinforce it and thereby drive more males into
migratory labor. In 1953, Richards returned to the Bemba
to find that 70% of the men were away.

These cases--Mossi, Ngoni, and Bemba--suggest that while
remittances may raise income levels, migration and remittances tend to become part of a broader, long-term
depressive economic trend for labor-exporting areas.
In his review of labor movements in Central Africa,
Mitchell (1962) finds that the pattern of labor migration
has not stabilized but rather *intensified* so that more
and more men need to migrate, thus depressing the rural
economy. Read's early study (1942) of migration in
Nyasaland notes some of the personal reasons for the
intensification of the migratory pattern:

> Men on their return are constantly comparing
> what they have seen and experienced... The
> women on the other hand, with certain exceptions,
> have had no opportunity of seeing standards of
> living different from those of their own
> neighbourhood... The situation then is one
> where many of the men are definitely aiming
> at a higher standard of living, but the dead
> weight of the women is pulling them back.
> This makes for friction in families, and the
> men's escape is to emigrate frequently.

Another inducement to go off again is the
malaise felt by the men who return with
money and want to use it profitably and
intelligently. There is a constant conflict
between their reputation among their friends
and relatives for generosity and their common
sense about the use of their new-found wealth.
In the more backward areas I found the majority
of returned emigrants pessimistic and despondent
about their economic future. (1942:629)

Plotnicov's research on Nigerian migrants (1965; see
1967) also notes that migrants often cannot meet the
expectations of their rural relatives and, even when
they wish to return home, the migrants remain away to
fulfill their obligations and to avoid the immediacy of
family pressures. Under such circumstances, Berg's
short-term analysis of migration and remittances should
be considered in a broader context.

It is important to examine the effects of migration and
remittances in terms of long-range trends and within
the context of wider transformations occurring in the
economy. Some of the best data documenting such trends
comes from Rhodesia. In the late nineteenth century,
colonial authorities suppressed warfare and the slave
trade in the Rhodesian area in order to secure a labor
force (Gann 1955); yet, through the early part of the
twentieth century, Rhodesians had to be forced to work
for colonial enterprises. In 1911, large-scale contract
labor was recruited in this manner from Northern Rhodesia
for work in the mines of Katanga; their deferred wages
remitted to Northern Rhodesia equaled the colony's
total domestic exports (Neumark 1964:93). Under this
system of coercive recruitment, wages were not a primary
concern, but as mining efforts shifted to the nearby
Copperbelt, migration from rural areas intensified as
labor demand began to take hold. The reason that labor
demand became operative at this time can be found, in
large part, in the worsening situation in the rural
areas. European land expropriation, taxation, and the
introduction of the plow (which accelerated soil erosion)
all hampered cash cropping (Wilson and Wilson 1945:20),
and a lack of economic alternatives helped to make
migration an economic necessity. At the same time,
incomes from migration, while among the lowest in
the world (Wilson 1941:37), were much higher than those
obtained in the rural areas, and hence personal income
rose for migrants' families in labor-exporting areas
(Turner and Turner 1955; see also Mitchell 1962;

14

Gluckman 1941). The Nyakyusa were among those groups to
benefit from migration. The Wilsons found:

> Nyakyusa prosperity partly depended on the
> fact that they lived near the Lupa goldfields,
> worked for short periods and took most of
> their earnings home. (1945:20)

Gulliver's later and more detailed study of the Nyakyusa
showed that food production suffered little, and the
money and goods brought back by the migrants more than
compensated for other losses (1957:69). Gulliver also
noted, however, that land shortages, low yields, and
falling crop prices compelled people to seek money
through migration. The land squeeze and continuing
cash shortages throughout rural Rhodesia gave rise to
a situation in which migration was necessary *regardless*
of wages paid or the labor needs of the mines (Arrighi
1970).

The Rhodesian case indicates that as migration continues,
a point may be reached where remittances cannot compensate for manpower losses, as the following passage
from the Keiskammahoek Rural Survey (South Africa)
illustrates:

> The people of this district are seen to be
> dependent upon the earnings of emigrants for
> their very existence, and it is poverty which
> forces them out to work. But this very exodus
> is itself a potent cause of the perpetuation
> of poverty at home, for the absence of so many
> in the prime of life inhibits economic progress
> and certainly accounts in no small measure for
> the low productivity of the district. In many
> cases land is not ploughed for the simple reason
> that there is no one to do the ploughing....
>   (Woddis 1962:26, see also Houghton
>   1952:1953)

Since the remaining people could not produce enough food
for themselves, they spent their remittances on imported
food. Agricultural production dropped below subsistence
requirements and remittances did not compensate for the
rise in the *real* cost of living.

The distinction between rising income and rises in the
real income is an important one, if only because some
studies seem to take income figures at face value. Given

the vexing problem of measuring cost of living in
underdeveloped economies, a reliance on income statistics
is understandable, but this emphasis may give the im-
pression that the standard of living is improving when
income relative to the cost of living--real income--is
actually declining (Easterlin n.d.). Incomes in underdeveloped areas are subject to inflationary trends and,
more significantly, *qualitative* changes in the way of
life, which cannot be precisely measured. Thus, during
periods of rising income, people may be purchasing *new*
goods which seem optional but may in time become necessary substitutes for older goods. As these goods become
indispensable, an increasing need for money is engendered
and, under these circumstances, it is difficult for real
income to keep pace (Arrighi 1970). In the early stages
of remittance dependence, real income frequently does
rise, while in the latter stages the cost of living in
a new economic environment may offset *relative* increases
in income.

There is the possibility that the migrant-labor system
can lead to an *absolute* decrease in real income for
remittance recipients. Guatemala offers one such case.
Despite the fact that per capita income for Guatemala
as a whole increased between 1950 and 1965, rural income
probably decreased absolutely over the same period of
time, and rural opportunities for peasants also decreased.
The decrease in income is correlated with a 50% increase
in the employment of migrant labor. The migrants make
less than full-time farm employees and peasants, and the
large plantations have opted for migrants in preference
to full-time employees, thereby cutting costs and enabling
further expansion of the plantations. Since displaced
full-time employees and other migrants make less in
absolute terms than they would have had they remained
either peasants or full-time plantation workers, remittances cannot offset the costs of migration, and thus the
whole rural economy suffers as migration increases (Adams
1970:390-394).

When considered on a case by case basis, it seems that
each of the three interpretations of the effects of
migration and remittances has both its strengths and
weaknesses. Berg's short-term view of costs and benefits
needs to be supplemented by a long-term, more comprehensive view of migration and remittances. A second
view--that "migratory wage labor may be a means of
securing income to support the *status quo* of societies
with faltering indigenous economies" (Gonzales 1969:

16

xiv-xv; see Gulliver 1955:36; Feindt and Browing
1972)--receives some support, but it should be amended
to note that, as migration and remittance dependence
intensify, the *status quo* itself is altered. The third
view, that migration and remittances contribute to
underdevelopment, receives a good deal of support and
nicely complements the other two interpretations. In
comparing these different interpretations, then, a more
synthetic approach suggests itself.

Generally speaking, migration seems to lead to an
increasing dependency on the wider economy and especially
on labor-importing areas. Whatever the initial causes
of migration (see DuToit 1975; Douglass 1970, 1971),
once the process is underway, it tends to perpetuate
itself. Although migration may appear voluntary, in
the sense of real economic alternatives, it is quite
often a necessary part of a new economic adaptation.
Local production may or may not decline markedly, depending on the nature and extent of migration (W. Watson
1958), the amount of money remitted (J.L. Watson 1975),
and the degree to which cash-crop production is discouraged or at least not encouraged (Myint 1964:61), but
the *need* for money usually increases, as does the rate
of unemployment. So, without migration and subsequent
remittances, many people would suffer privation
(Gulliver 1955:35; Berg 1965:180; Caldwell 1969:152-153).
While acknowledging that remittances do speed the process
of monetization and therefore initially raise income and
consumption levels (Caldwell 1969:216), the migrant-
labor system has not led to economic growth in labor-
exporting areas. Instead it has perpetuated a pattern
of low income and low productivity (Myint 1964:64).
There are no examples of countries that have developed
through migration and remittances.

The primary beneficiaries of the migrant-labor system
are the developed, labor-importing areas (Berg 1965:178).
It is they who are developing more rapidly in both
relative and absolute terms (McNamara 1972). The
widening income and opportunity gap that makes migration
attractive to people in underdeveloped areas also makes
migrant labor attractive to developed areas. As long as
differential income and employment opportunities exist
and as long as there is a demand for unskilled labor,
wage-labor migration will persist (Todaro 1969). The
dependence of labor-exporting areas on migration for a
substantial part of their income makes their own rate
of growth almost irrelevant, since the greater the income
differential and the fewer the local opportunities, the

17

greater the incentive for migration. The crucial rate
of growth lies in the advanced, labor-importing areas
where relatively cheap migrant labor helps to increase
productivity (Jones and Smith 1970) and speeds capital
accumulation more quickly than would have been possible
without migrant labor (Kindleberger 1967).

This interpretation of the differential economic effects
of migration and remittances on underdeveloped areas is
less positive than the interpretations of Miracle and
Berry (1970) and Gugler (1968). These authors discuss
how migration and remittances promote human capital and
entrepreneurial activities in underdeveloped areas, and
how migration increases the flow of new ideas. While
such effects are important, they do not usually alter
the underdeveloped nature and dependent character of
labor-exporting areas. A report in the *OECD Observer*
states that returning migrants do not contribute to
development:

> In no way do the returning migrants help further
> their country's growth, whether by the use of
> the savings they have accumulated or the ex-
> perience they have acquired. (in A. Ward 1975:34)

The very fact that remittances may provide a higher
standard of living can actually discourage local enterprise. In his study of an emigrant community in Hong
Kong, J.L. Watson found:

> The emigrant remittances are sufficient in most
> cases to support the villagers at a higher
> standard of living, and very few are willing
> to work for the meager wages offered in the
> knitting shops... Even if these handicraft
> enterprises had been more successful *they could
> not have rivaled emigration as an alternative
> occupation* for the male villagers... The village
> leaders would like to introduce more remunerative
> forms of employment; but they realize that,
> politically and economically, the problem is
> beyond their control (1975:156-157, emphasis added).

In agricultural communities, migration and remittances
can act as disincentives to production, although this
is by no means inevitable. There is even some evidence
that dependence on migration and remittances can be
reduced without severe disruptions. In rural India,
migration by the agricultural classes was slowed by
improvements in agricultural technology that required

18

increased labor inputs (Mamdani 1972:105-127).
Nevertheless, the more usual relationship between
migration, remittances, and underdevelopment requires
continued migration and leaves labor-exporting areas
vulnerable to wider economic trends.

Remittance-dependent economies are highly sensitive to
changes in international economic conditions. During
the depression of the 1930s, Chen Han-sheng found a
Chinese emigrant community adjusting its pattern of
remittance expenditure and migration to world economic
conditions. He notes that

> with the world economic depression and the
> corresponding improvement in the Chinese
> exchange rate, remittances from Chinese overseas
> have suddenly and greatly increased. To be
> more specific, thousands of Taishan's sons in
> the United States and elsewhere have, in
> addition to their usual remittances for the
> support of relatives at home, sent large sums
> for investment in their home community or
> neighborhood; and since the times were unpro-
> pitious for industrial or other forms of
> capitalistic enterprise, a large part of
> these savings found its way into land
> purchases, producing something of a boom...
> Another reason for the abnormal rent increases
> in this region is that, also as a result of
> the world economic depression, many small
> Chinese businessmen or truck gardeners could
> no longer make a living abroad and decided to
> come home. The return of large numbers of
> these men undoubtedly raised the demand for
> use of land, whether by purchase or lease,
> producing yet another--more direct if
> smaller--tendency to raise rents. (1936:67-68)

The economic vulnerability of remittance-dependent areas
may be reflected in other ways. In the Hong Kong village
of San Tin, whose members depend almost entirely on
remittances from villagers working in Chinese restaurants
in London halfway around the world, J.L. Watson comments
that

> this regular flow of remittances is so critical
> that even a brief disruption would cause
> immediate hardship to almost every household
> in the village. As a result, much
> gossip in San Tin involves rumors of

> non-remitting sons or husbands. The villagers
> understandably are concerned that their
> breadwinners might stop sending money home....
> (1974:219)

Dependence on remittances for income in labor-exporting
areas is precarious and economically viable only as long
as migration and remittances continue. When either
migration or remittances, or both, are diminished or
halted, the real nature of labor-exporting economies
is brought to the fore. One area currently feeling
the effects of a slowdown is southern Italy. Labor
markets in Germany and Switzerland have sharply curbed
Italian migration to the point where many migrants are
now returning. Southern Italy was extremely dependent
on these migrants for its income; the average agricultural income was $400, while the average remittance
income was $800 (Halevy 1972). Now, with remittances
decreasing and migrants returning, the old problems--
land shortages, acute poverty, social and political
unrest--are reappearing. A similar situation is
occurring in parts of West Africa (Caldwell 1969:152-153)
and Mexico (Foster 1967:287-288). Thus the remittance
system may mask the underdeveloped nature of these
economies, and when the system collapses, the ensuing
economic crunch can have very severe consequences.

From this overview, it appears that, on the family and
individual level, migration and remittances may offer a
partial solution to the problem of underdevelopment.
The intensifying pattern of migration and remittance
dependence, however, is symptomatic of underdevelopment
on the structural level. Furthermore, as migration and
remittance dependence become more important at the
national and local levels, they tend to make labor-
exporting economies more vulnerable to wider economic
trends, including inflation and depression, thereby
exacerbating and perpetuating underdevelopment.

The remainder of this study attempts to apply this
synthetic perspective to islands in the Pacific Basin,
where a number of territories and countries have recently
entered the migrant-labor system. Although this area
still conjures up visions of a tropical paradise sup-
porting a primitive economy, in fact, the islands fall
very much within the orbit of other underdeveloped areas
(Fairbairn 1971b). Two-thirds of these island groups
have per capita incomes of $140 or less (Salter 1970:22).
Plagued with many of the problems of other underdeveloped

areas, the islands are further hampered by smallness, geographical isolation, and lack of regional integration (R. Ward 1967). In the post-war era, these predominantly export-oriented economies have experienced declines in agricultural trade, and migration is increasingly used as a means of obtaining income. A limiting case is provided by the islands of Wallis and Futuna, tiny territories under French rule:

> Before World War II, both Wallis and Futuna produced copra (an average of 1500 tons per annum); but the Wallis palms have been ravaged by the rhinocerous beetle and although eradication work has been carried out and progress has been made in rehabilitating native plantations, no copra was exported in 1967. In 1966 about 100 tons of copra were exported from the Futuna group.

> Chief means of livelihood, apart from subsistence agriculture, are government employment and money sent back to their families by the many Wallis islanders who have gone to work in New Caledonia. (*Pacific Islands Yearbook* 1968:265)

To a lesser extent, the sequence of agricultural decline, labor migration, and remittance dependence can be found in American Samoa, Tonga, the Cooks, the Tokelaus, Niue, the American Trust Territory, and the French Trust Territory, among others. Western Samoa also falls within this group, and it is to Western Samoa that we shall now turn.

3 Migration, Remittances, and Underdevelopment in Western Samoa

Western Samoa had been experiencing underdevelopment
long before migration and remittances became integral
parts of its economy. The details of the islands'
economic history are now well documented (Stanner
1953; Stace 1956; Lewthwaite 1962; Davidson 1967;
Gilson 1970; Pitt 1970; Lockwood 1971), but a brief
review of Samoan underdevelopment will provide a back-
ground for an understanding of the impact of migration
and remittances in this particular case.

There is little disagreement about Western Samoa's
underdeveloped condition. Of the 17 underdeveloped
countries participating in the Asian Development Bank's
(ADB) regional seminar on agriculture in 1969, Western
Samoa shared with South Vietnam and Indonesia the dubious
distinction of having a negative compound growth-rate
per year in agricultural exports and in total exports
during the years 1957/1959 through 1964/1966. It had
the highest percentage of agricultural imports (56%)
of any of the ADB member nations (Ojala 1969:59, 62)
and its population growth rate continues to be one of
the highest in the world. In 1971, the United Nations
identified Western Samoa as one of the 16 poorest
countries in the world. In 1975, the islands were
classified among the world's "worst economic hardship
cases," the so-called "Fourth World," including Haiti,
Lesotho, and Bangladesh (*Newsweek*, September 15, 1975,
page 38).

Such comparative data, although suggestive, may be
misleading for it provides little in the way of context
for understanding Western Samoa's economic situation.
More helpful are the general trends in production,

22

income, and consumption *within* Western Samoa since the
turn of the century. Although precise data are not
available, certain trends are nevertheless discernible.
First of all, time-series data from 1900 through 1956
show that levels of production in agricultural exports
have "increased merely enough to restore production
standards obtaining fifty years ago, and not enough, by
some 18%, to reach the position ruling in the nineteen
twenties" (Stace 1956:71). Between 1956 and 1972, per
capita production of agricultural exports declined to
levels *below* those at the turn of the twentieth century.
While the *basis* of agricultural export production in
copra, cocoa, and bananas has been broadened over the
last 70 years to include more and more of the Samoan
population, productivity itself has declined. Second,
incomes from agriculture increased sharply following
World War II, but in the last decade they have fallen
sharply (see Table 1). Third, consumption has increased steadily, causing the trade and payments
deficits that are common in underdeveloped countries.
From these trends, it is possible to view Western Samoa's
economy as deteriorating--underdeveloping, if you will--
in terms of itself. The little development that has
occurred has been concentrated in the hands of Europeans
and, to a lesser extent, part-Europeans (Fairbairn 1971a).

The history of underdevelopment in Western Samoa began
more than a century ago. Although it may be difficult
to conceive of South Sea islanders undergoing the same
historical transformations as those of people in Asia,
Africa, and Latin America, the Samoan economy did pass
from a stage of *un*development, in which local factors
of production and redistribution were dominant, to a
stage of *under*development, relative to the larger economy
into which it was incorporated and in which foreign
factors of production and redistribution were dominant.
The establishment of a European export enclave in the
mid-nineteenth century with new land and labor interests
brought numerous changes to the Samoan economy (Gilson
1970; Lewthwaite 1962; Davidson 1967), although the consequences of German, British, American, and finally New
Zealand colonial influence in Western Samoa were nowhere
as damaging as in other parts of the world, including
other parts of the Pacific (Valentine 1970). The Samoans
were never defeated in battle and, due largely to the
existence of an indigenous hierarchical structure and
the exigencies of indirect rule, an early, if troubled,
mutual accommodation was worked out.

TABLE 1:

PER CAPITA AGRICULTURAL EXPORT VALUES
FOR WESTERN SAMOA,
1946 - 1972

Year	Index*
1946	100
1947	182
1948	146
1949	168
1950	155
1951	195
1952	195
1953	207
1954	225
1955	254
1956	182
1957	182
1958	271
1959	292
1960	240
1961	160
1962	230
1963	230
1964	197
1965	155
1966	121
1967**	114
1968	135
1969	144
1970	104
1971	124
1972	80

* Based on the 1946 index of 100 = £10.4.

** 1967 to 1972 index based on a conversion of Western
Samoan pounds to Western Samoan dollars, where
£2 = $WS 1.00. In 1970, $WS 1.00 = $US 0.70; in
1972, $WS 1.00 = $US 0.60.

Under a paradigm of benevolent paternalism, the Samoans were incorporated into a state-level polity and an agricultural-export economy. The stability of the initial Samoan adaptation to the wider world has given this relatively recent social situation an aura of "tradition." Indeed, the Western Samoans pride themselves on the retention of Samoan custom or *fa'asamoa*, but a closer look at *fa'asamoa* reveals that it is more an ideology of tradition than a behavioral replica of pre-European society. What is referred to as *fa'asamoa* today probably has as its basis the Samoan-mission-trader equilibrium that developed between 1830 and 1870 (Keesing 1934: 476; Stanner 1953:305-323).

Where cultural continuity has been maintained, it has been within the context of foreign control. The conservative *fa'asamoa* ethos can be viewed as a product of underdevelopment, and it might be expected that, as development occurs, the conscious model of *fa'asamoa* will disappear. In fact, this is what has happened. In underdeveloped Western Samoa, the people speak of developed American Samoa as having lost the Samoan way, while American Samoans point to Western Samoa's poverty as a vehicle that has preserved *fa'asamoa*. Firth has noted phenomena similar to *fa'asamoa* in other parts of the Pacific, stating that

> consciousness of the changes in so many
> spheres may lead, as in Polynesian societies,
> to a renewed emphasis on traditional or
> modified (pseudo-) traditional forms, which
> are as it were obtruded as evidence of a social
> solidarity which may in fact be threatened or
> lost in other fields. (1963b:88)

Thus the persistence of *fa'asamoa* can be traced to an absence of development beginning in the mid-nineteenth century.

In a sense, it is misleading to speak of the Western Samoan economy and Samoan underdevelopment without reference to the wider economy and to specific historical circumstances. As a colony and then as a trust territory, Western Samoa had little control over most of the political and economic decisions that affected its economic situation. Furthermore, despite its political independence since 1962, Western Samoa continues to be strongly influenced by the outside world.

With the promise of independence following World War II,
the United Nations and New Zealand began to carefully
investigate economic conditions in the islands. The
first of Western Samoa's postwar observers, W.E.H.
Stanner, reported that the basic tools for assessing
the state of the economy--a reliable census and economic
survey--were lacking. More disturbingly, he noted that
while the territory was politically quite advanced, on
available economic evidence it would have to be put

> in a subclass so 'backward' that the problem is
> still one of creating most of the conditions
> precedent to development. (Stanner 1953:409)

As information became available through policy-oriented
studies conducted in the 1950s (Stace 1956; Fox and
Cumberland 1962), it was generally agreed that an
underdeveloped Western Samoa would be hard pressed to
break out of the trap of low income and rising population, thus facing increasingly severe economic
hardship in future decades. The economic record of
the first 50 years of the twentieth century provided
little encouragement. Although some observers emphasized population constraints on development (Pirie and
Barrett 1962) while others emphasized social and institutional barriers (Ala'ilima and Ala'ilima 1965), there
was a broad consensus as to the underdeveloped state of
the economy.

In the late 1950s and early 1960s, the seriousness of
the Western Samoan economic situation was still a matter
of debate. On the one hand, there were those who felt
that better times lay ahead. To them the situation did
not seem acute, as it rarely does in countries living
under conditions of "tropical affluence" (Fisk 1962).
In these countries, underdevelopment does not entail
the kind of poverty that is found in countries with
acute land shortages, chronic food shortages, high
infant-mortality rates, and short life spans. In each
of these respects, Western Samoa was relatively well
off. The slow economic decline that had occurred over
the last half-century was not regarded with alarm
because its effects were not catastrophic. Hope was
not abandoned because fairly rapid growth is possible
in such economies (Epstein 1968; Salisbury 1970; Fisk
and Shand 1969), and since there was growth in the 1950s,
it was natural to expect continuing economic good fortune.

On the other hand, there were the pessimists--those
experts, both Samoan and foreign, who expected a change

26

for the worse. They predicted that the conditions that
had led to decline were likely to continue, and that
the expansion of the 1950s would be offset by increasing
consumption, leading to balance-of-payments problems
that would extend through the 1960s. In one prophetic
analysis, a United Nations official warned:

> A combination of unfortunate circumstances
> in weather, plant diseases, pests, and poor
> world market prices for two or even three
> of the major crops could result in a financial
> crisis for the Samoan nation. (Gerakas 1964:33)

The optimists, however, were not deterred, especially
the popular press. In 1964, BOOM IS ON THE WAY headlined
an article in the *Pacific Islands Monthly*. The same
caption appeared in an editorial in *Samoana*, a Samoan
newspaper, on January 26, 1966. An opinion was offered
that things were not as bad as they seemed:

> In fact, indications are that this country is
> on the verge of a boom that in five or six
> years could transform its economy from that
> of subsistence to one of the most flourishing
> in the South Pacific.

The following week, Western Samoa was devastated by the
worst hurricane in the South Pacific in 75 years. The
hurricane underscored the vulnerability of the economy
in a manner that left few illusions. The experts had
been correct, and in the five-year period of 1964 to
1969, Western Samoa was to be visited by all of the
woes prophesized. Hurricanes struck in 1966 and again
in 1968. The important banana industry, already decimated
by bunchy-top virus, was almost eliminated. The hurricanes curtailed production of the other two major export
crops, copra and cocoa. Fortunately, world prices did
not seriously affect Western Samoa until the early 1970s.
Although copra production rebounded dramatically, falling
prices led to new lows in agricultural revenues. Trade
deficits persisted through this period and, by the
mid-1970s, the trade and payments situation had reached
the point of near fiscal crisis.

IMPORTANCE OF REMITTANCES

It was during the 1960s, when agricultural production
and agricultural incomes in Western Samoa declined
sharply, that remittances became an important source

27

of revenue. By 1966, it was estimated that 8% of the
population born in Western Samoa had migrated overseas
on a permanent basis (Lockwood 1971:26), with an equal
percentage overseas on a temporary basis. The remittances sent back by this 16% of the population provided
about 30% of the *national* income in 1966; their contribution to *personal* income was even higher. In 1974, it
was estimated that 20% of the Western Samoan population
was living overseas and remitting more than 50% of the
national income. When viewed as a third sector, next
to the agricultural and government sectors in the
Samoan economy, the migrants were, and continue to be,
the most productive sector in terms of personal revenue
generated. They are indeed Western Samoa's "most
valuable export."

Although government and academic reports[1] from the 1960s
mention remittances, these reports were generally concerned with migration as an "economic escape valve" to
alleviate Western Samoa's employment and population
problems. The *Economic Development Programme* for
1966-1970 concluded that unless overseas labor markets
opened up, the number of Samoans migrating would be
too small to have any marked effect on the employment
problem or on population growth. Yet, even the
relatively small number of migrants and their remittances were already having a substantial impact on the
Samoan *economy*.

One area of impact was the islands' balance of trade.
In the past, when there was little capital investment
or colonial funding, the local cash economy was regulated
almost entirely by production of agricultural exports
for the world market. People could only purchase imported goods with the money earned directly or indirectly
from agriculture, and any decline in agricultural
earnings automatically resulted in a decline in import
demand. By the late 1950s and 1960s, declines in agricultural earnings occurred *without* a subsequent fall in
import demand. In fact, demand increased, leading to
severe balance-of-trade deficits. This trend clearly
implied the existence of surplus money; increased savings
and large amounts of money in circulation seemed to
confirm the existence of a surplus. While some of this

---

[1] See Gerakas (1964); Government of Western Samoa
(1968:1-2); Davidson (1967:418); Pitt (1970:154-189);
Lockwood (1971); and McArthur (1964).

surplus came from loans, the sale of overseas holdings, and other types of 'invisible' bank transfers, most of it came from personal remittances.

While remittances have become a very significant part of the Western Samoan economy, apart from general acknowledgments of migration and remittances, Fairbairn's article (1961) is the only study to detail one part of the rather complex remittance system. Perhaps one reason for this is that much of the information is un-available or incomplete, and even this information may be inaccurate. The remainder of this chapter will attempt to summarize the crucial dimensions of the system: the number and kind of migrants, the number and kind of remitters, the value and distribution of remittances, and their impact.

MIGRATION TO AMERICAN SAMOA AND NEW ZEALAND

Total out-migration from Western Samoa, both permanent and temporary, has been steadily increasing over the last two-and-one-half decades with American Samoa and New Zealand being the primary labor markets. During World War II, estimated departures of Samoans from Western Samoa fluctuated between 2,000 and 3,500 annually, although the net outflow was more than offset by migration to the islands from American Samoa through 1951 (Stace 1956:4). By the early 1950s, total depar-tures had more than doubled, net out-migration from Western Samoa was beginning to take hold, and remit-tances were becoming a source of income for the islands. Fairbairn calculated that by 1954 the cost of migration to New Zealand was exceeded by remittances from New Zealand (1961:28), and that year can be used as a some-what arbitrary date for the beginning of the era of remittance dependence in Western Samoa. Tables 2 and 3 present the data on departures and net migration with a breakdown by point of destination for the period 1954 through 1972.

Total out-migration increased more than threefold during this period. Most migrants moved back and forth between Western Samoa and nearby American Samoa. The relative proximity and accessibility of American Samoa, coupled with the fact that most Western Samoans have relatives there, made this United States territory a popular visiting spot, and the recipient of about 80% of Western Samoa's migrants. An inexpensive (albeit nauseating) boatride available several times weekly

TABLE 2:

DEPARTURES FROM WESTERN SAMOA BY
WESTERN SAMOANS, 1954-1972

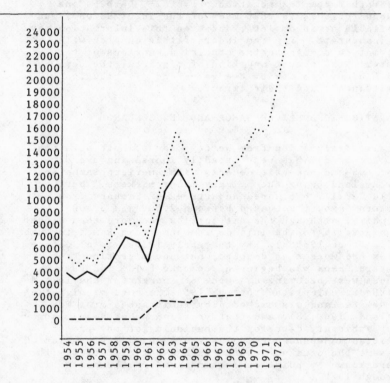

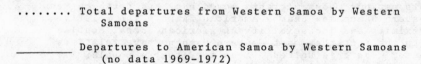

.... Total departures from Western Samoa by Western
          Samoans

_____ Departures to American Samoa by Western Samoans
          (no data 1969-1972)

-------- Departures to New Zealand by Western Samoans
          (no data 1967-1972)

TABLE 3:

NET MIGRATION FROM WESTERN SAMOA
BY WESTERN SAMOANS, 1954-1969

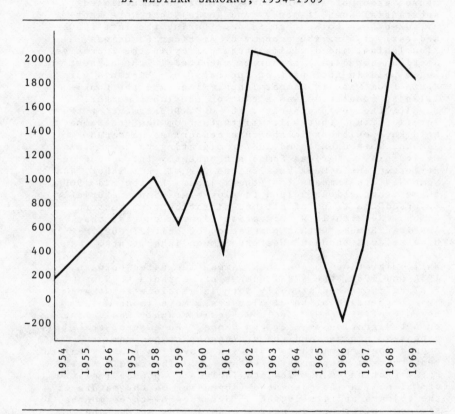

and regularly scheduled Polynesian Airlines flights made
it fairly easy for people to commute between the two
Samoas. Gifts received while visiting American Samoa
were brought back as remittances, usually in small
amounts.

American Samoa was also a major source of remittances
through wage labor, as a small and more-or-less permanent group of Western Samoan laborers accumulated
substantial sums of money (and goods) that were sent
or taken back to Western Samoa. During the late 1950s
and early 1960s, the economy of American Samoa was
flourishing, and a minimum-wage policy in the lucrative,
American-owned tuna canneries resulted in the highest
wages paid in that part of the Pacific. Migrants were
drawn from Western Samoa, Tonga, Niue, and the Cook
Islands; soon there was a glut on the labor market.
Despite the new prosperity, the U.S. Department of the
Interior found that while migrants from Western Samoa
held key positions in the tuna canneries, American
Samoans were unemployed and/or migrating to Hawaii and
California. American Samoa subsequently introduced re-
strictive employment regulations for migrant labor, and
some Western Samoans lost their jobs. By the mid-1960s,
these restrictions helped to slow migration and briefly
reversed the trend of net out-migration from Western
Samoa. Nevertheless, migration figures suggest that
American Samoa, with a population of only 27,000, may
have several thousand Western Samoan inhabitants.

While migration to American Samoa fluctuated between
1954 and 1968, the small number of migrants to New
Zealand increased steadily both in absolute terms and
as a percentage of total migrants. More importantly,
net migration to New Zealand became roughly equivalent
to net migration to American Samoa. Because of the
expenses involved and the stringency of government
regulations on migrants, Samoans traveling to New Zealand
tend to be a much more select group. The requirements
for migration to New Zealand include a sponsor (relative
or friend), a job guarantee (depending on the nature of
the sojourn and its degree of permanence--three months,
six months, or permanent), a housing guarantee, and
clearance by the respective governments. These requirements lead to longer stays, a higher rate of employment,
much higher incomes, and more money for remittances.
The necessity of having a sponsor, who may also provide
housing, help to procure a job, and pay the fares,
encourages a situation in which "chain migration" is the
norm; that is, relatives will sponsor other relatives

who will in turn sponsor still other relatives--a pattern analogous to the European migrations to the United States in the early twentieth century. Given the regulations surrounding migration, the often lengthy and complex bureaucratic procedures, the high costs of travel, and the exigencies of adapting to New Zealand life, family relationships take on special importance and may be severely strained at a time when kinsmen are providing the auspices of migration. Intergovernmental relations may also be strained.

The increasing number of Western Samoan migrants to New Zealand has made both governments sensitive to certain questions regarding the migrant population. There are waiting lists for potential migrants, and Western Samoa, faced with a population that is rapidly expanding, has been negotiating with New Zealand to allow for further migration. Yet New Zealand is con- fronted with similar pressures from other island groups, including Fiji, Tonga, the Tokelaus, the Cooks, and Niue, some of whose residents are New Zealand citizens and who therefore receive priority over Samoans and other islanders. The Western Samoans view this as a question of discrimination; the New Zealand Government views it in a slightly different light. Aside from the economic problems and the fact that, next to the Maori, the Samoans are the largest non-European group in New Zealand, the New Zealand Government sees the Samoans as a potential source of social problems: crime, juvenile delinquency, and welfare. A recent manifes- tation of the intergovernmental tensions involving Samoan migrants occurred in 1970 when New Zealand found that many of Western Samoa's single female migrants were pregnant on arriving in New Zealand; New Zealand authorities issued a warning that it would conduct pregnancy tests thereafter. Western Samoan officials responded with a statement about discriminatory policies against Samoans and about affronts to the honor of Samoan women as well as women in general. Although this incident may seem trivial, it is not, because single females are regarded as the most reliable remitters, and curtailing their migration could hurt Western Samoa economically.

The composition of migrants to New Zealand has been changing recently. The greater expense and the more complicated maneuvering required for migration to New Zealand has, in the past, favored part-Samoans and Samoans residing in the port town of Apia. Prior to 1950, most of the migrants were "mixed-bloods" or

33

"half-castes," part-Samoans who comprise about 10% of
the population of Western Samoa and who are more likely
to be better educated, wealthier, English speaking,
and Euro-American oriented as a result of being the
offspring of mixed unions. It was not until the early
1950s that the "full-bloods" or "real" Samoans, as they
sometimes designate themselves, became the predominant
migrant group; they constitute about 89% of an estimated
Western Samoan population of 155,000 (as of 1975).
Migrants from this group tend to resemble part-Samoans
more than their "full-blooded" village counterparts,
although Samoan villagers, too, are migrating in increasing numbers.

The migrant population numbers in the tens of thousands
with perhaps as many as 30,000 Western Samoans living
abroad on a permanent or temporary basis. Most of
these migrants live in New Zealand, with a few thousand
in American Samoa and several hundred elsewhere. The
demographic consequences of their absence are reflected
in the Western Samoan census materials. In the five-year
age groupings between 20 and 44, during the period 1961
to 1971, the rate of population growth was markedly
lower for both males and females than in groups under
20 and over 44; in some of the intermediate age brackets,
there has been an absolute decrease in population.

Migration has led a slowing of the rate of population
growth for the islands as a whole. For example, between
1966 and 1971, there should have been an overall increase in the population of 16%, but, due largely to
migration, there was an increase of only 9.3%. Ordinarily,
the loss of manpower from critical age groups through
migration could effect levels of agricultural production.
Yet the exodus of the 1950s and 1960s did not seem to
have cut into the islands' agricultural labor force in
most areas (Fairbairn 1967), primarily because most
migrants have tended to come from the Apia area rather
than rural agricultural areas, and because the sex ratio
of the migrants was fairly balanced rather than being
heavily weighted in favor of males. While the migrant
exodus had not yet aggravated agricultural production,
it offered at best only a temporary solution to rapid
population growth. Meanwhile, the deterioration of the
agricultural sector and the overall decline of the
Western Samoan economy continued to act as spurs to
migration.

Samoans prefer to migrate to New Zealand, primarily due
to economic considerations. Migrants to New Zealand

are likely to make more money than their counterparts in
American Samoa and are therefore more likely to send
large remittances. This is because New Zealand encourages employment and pays very high wages, among the
highest in the world. The structural economic significance of differences in opportunity and income between
Western Samoa and New Zealand can be appreciated by
noting that there are more Samoans employed in industry
in New Zealand than there are in Western Samoa. The
average Samoan laborer in New Zealand can make many
times what he could make back in the islands; a rural
Samoan migrant can make the equivalent of ten years'
income in Western Samoa during a single year in New
Zealand. Higher living costs and expenses will defray
most of this income, but a relatively large amount will
remain for remittances. Although not all migrants send
or bring remittances (especially long-time, permanent
migrants), the close family ties that led to sponsorship
of migration are likely to be honored through the
sending of remittances.

Migration to American Samoa is relatively inexpensive
and usually does not involve employment. Because people
are visiting relatives for a short time, opportunities
for gathering large sums of money for remittances are
far fewer than in New Zealand, but remittances from
laborers in American Samoa, particularly because of
their proximity, can be considerable. Those Western
Samoans who are employed in American Samoa have a much
higher income than their counterparts in Western Samoa,
although much lower than Samoans in New Zealand. Thus,
while American Samoa receives most of Western Samoa's
migrants and provides some remittances, in terms of
providing opportunities for larger remittances, American
Samoa cannot compare with New Zealand.

The magnitude of difference in amounts remitted between
American Samoa and New Zealand is not known due to
differences in monitoring systems. New Zealand remittances are closely monitored, whereas American
remittances are not. At present, Western Samoan
migrants in New Zealand are confined to using postal
and banking channels when forwarding remittances, thereby
facilitating a closer monitoring of their volume and
value. Prior to 1967, formal channels could be bypassed
and large amounts of money left New Zealand and arrived
in the island unmonitored. Western Samoans frequently
sent cash directly through the mails, rather than by
money order, or they brought it in on their persons,
occasionally by the suitcaseful. Then New Zealand

canceled its overseas currency-exchange privileges and
tightened its American currency-exchange policy, which
prevented islanders from converting New Zealand currency to American currency and then remitting it.
Although sporadic traffic in New Zealand currency can
still be found in Western Samoa, most funds that pass
between New Zealand and Western Samoa are now accounted
for.

On the other hand, American remittances are unmonitored.
The direct cash flows from American Samoa and the United
States are not known, but their magnitude is sufficient
to make American money a second currency in Western
Samoa. American remittances often pass through the
Western Samoan banking system; however, they are not
monitored for place of origin and much of the cash
never enters banking channels. Although the total value
of remittances passing through official channels can be
estimated, the total value of all remittances and their
points of origin are not known. Nevertheless, since
the New Zealand system is well monitored, crude minimal
estimates can be made for the remittance system as a
whole.

REMITTANCE INCOMES: VALUE AND DISTRIBUTION

The data on personal remittances as a portion of the
national income are quite limited. In part, this is
because national-income accounts were not kept until
the 1960s and because even in these accounts, it is
not always easy to discern distributional patterns.
Nevertheless, during the 1960s, remittances increased
as migration increased. Table 4 presents income data
on estimated remittances and on agricultural income
between 1964 and 1973. Although these figures show
that remittances are a sizeable part of total agricultural and remittance income, and hence national
income, one modification in the figures is necessary
for a more accurate estimate--the addition of *unmonitored*
remittances. For the year 1966, another $WS 350,000
at the very least, should be included. On a per capita
basis, remittance income would then be $WS 11. The
real significance of this small figure becomes apparent
when it is contrasted to gross per capita agricultural
income, about $WS 25 in 1966, meaning that remittances
constituted about 30% of the total combined agricultural

36

TABLE 4:

REMITTANCE INCOME FOR WESTERN SAMOA,
1964-1973*

YEAR	ESTIMATED VALUE OF MONITORED REMITTANCE INCOME (IN WS$)	TOTAL VALUE OF AGRICULTURAL EXPORTS (IN WS$)	REMITTANCES AS A PERCENTAGE OF REMITTANCE AND AGRICULTURAL INCOME
1964	690,000	5,046,000	12%
1965	1,009,000	4,167,000	20%
1966	1,120,600	3,295,000	25%
1967	993,600	3,139,000	24%
1968	791,800	3,838,000	17%
1969	1,000,000	4,212,000	19%
1970	1,700,000	3,349,000	34%
1971	1,900,000	4,484,000	30%
1972	2,500,000	3,356,000	43%
1973	3,600,000	3,785,000	49%

*estimates based on data from the Treasury Department,
Government of Western Samoa

Note: Most of the gross monitored remittances are
personal remittances, although this category
includes such diverse items as: gifts to and
from local persons to and from persons overseas,
grants from private sources to persons or
institutions in Western Samoa (i.e., churches),
payment and receipt of legacies, personal
receipts, personal transfer payments, and
other sums that may not fall under the rubric
of personal remittances as used here. The
remittance figures are subject to some error.

and remittance income for that year.[2] For the years
1967, 1968, and 1969, the estimates, including unmonitored remittances, would run between 21% and 28%,
not including remitted commodities; for 1970 and 1971,
the estimates would be about 37%. For 1973, total
remittances would exceed 50%.

These income estimates offer a very general picture of
the income situation in Western Samoa. In terms of the
actual distribution of income, other considerations are
involved. On the one hand, the majority of Samoans
living in villages are earning considerably less than
the "average Samoan." The 80% of the population living
in villages and producing 75% of the value of agricultural exports (Fairbairn 1970a:54) do not receive
an equivalent value in receipts because of marketing
and processing costs and taxation. Receipts for village
agriculturalists may be as high as 60% of the export
value of some crops and as low as 10% in the case of
cocoa (Pitt 1970:59n.2). On the other hand, the nonagricultural portion of the population, centered in
town, is earning much more than the "average Samoan."
A more meaningful characterization of each sector's
income can be obtained by employing net rather than
gross figures, by using paid-to-producer prices rather
than f.o.b. export prices, and by taking into account
the structural economic differences between town and
rural areas. Similar disaggregation procedures should
also be applied to remittance income, for unless
national-income statistics are disaggregated and their
distribution plotted, they can yield only very rough
information on the value of different kinds of income.

Within the national-income statistics, there is one type
of remittance that can be accurately measured and easily
mapped--money orders. A more refined estimate of distributional patterns can be derived from an examination
of money orders. They are an almost ideal form of remittances for the purposes of this study. Money orders
make up a large portion of the total monitored remittances,

---

[2]The average remittances per consumption unit for
14 villages located on the northwest coast of Upolu were
29% of total income in 1966. Thus, the 30% figure does
not seem unreasonable. The 14 villages are Utuali'i
(Lockwood 1971) and the 13 villages and sub-villages
surveyed by Bryant (1966).

they are accurately monitored, and the bulk are addressed
by village. Furthermore, money orders are now an almost
"pure" form of remittance in the sense that they are
mostly receipts as opposed to payments. Table 5 indicates the very sharp increase in the number and value
of money orders, especially during the past decade.

Money orders come almost exclusively from New Zealand,
and in 1969 they comprised almost one-half of the gross
monitored personal remittances ($WS 466,040 of an esti-
mated $WS 1,000,000). Money orders are of two types:
money-order telegrams (class 7) and regular money orders
(class 2). Money-order telegrams are the most common
type; they arrive more quickly, are more costly, and
may include a message to the receiver at additional
expense. Regular money orders are sometimes used by
foreign philatelists who purchase the interesting stamps
printed by the Western Samoan Government. Of about
4,600 regular money orders paid in 1969 (out of a total
of 21,252 money orders), almost 1,900 went for stamps
or similar kinds of business transactions. The remainder
were personal remittances to Samoans.

The average amount remitted per money order was $WS 22 in
1969, ranging from almost nothing to several hundred
dollars. The size of remittances is limited by an
official New Zealand ceiling on the amount that a remitter
can send to his relatives at any one time. One rationale
for this ceiling is that Samoans might send all their
money home and then have nothing left for themselves in
New Zealand. This rationale does not seem to be based
on the realities of Samoan economic behavior; nevertheless, the New Zealand Government requires clearance on
large money orders at the post-office level and
occasionally, for very large sums, at the national
banking level. These clearances are usually formalities
and, at worst, there may be several days delay in receiving clearance, but to a Samoan who does not speak
English well and who does not fully comprehend the
workings of a bureaucracy, this may be an embarrassment.
One means of avoiding clearance problems if an individual
does wish to send a large-sized money order is to send
it in smaller amounts, usually between $WS 20 and 40,
through several post offices.

The distribution of money orders to Western Samoans is
shown in Table 6. The operation of the money-order
system makes for some minor distortions in the actual
distribution of cash from money orders. Villagers will
sometimes have money orders sent to relatives in town

TABLE 5:

MONEY ORDERS:
VOLUME AND VALUE, 1958-1972

Year	Total number of money orders paid	Total value of money orders paid ($WS)
1958	3459	103,716
1959	3706	112,980
1960	4374	151,180
1961	6037	222,058
1962	4640	125,230
1963	4689	150,008
1964	5790	182,300
1965	6796	216,526
1966	14243	391,040
1967	21004	544,181
1968	17671	384,475
1969	21252	466,040
1970	30592	677,423
1971	31411	839,190
1972	36956	958,787

Source: Post Office Department, Government of Western
Samoa

TABLE 6:

DISTRIBUTION OF MONEY ORDERS
BY AREA, 1969

	Class 7 money-order telegrams	Class 2 money orders	Total money orders	Percent to area	Percent of population
Apia area*	6829	2707	9536	49%	20%
Upolu outside Apia area	7848	----	7848	41%	52%
Savaii	1957	----	1957	10%	28%

*Census area.

Note: This table presents only those money orders
       going to Western Samoans; the 1900 going
       for stamps or other business transactions
       are not included.

rather than to themselves because people in Apia have
easy access to the only money-order conversion center
on the island of Upolu. (Until 1970 the post offices
in Apia and in Tuasivi, Savaii, were the only places
where money orders could be cashed.) The urbanites
would then redistribute the money to their rural
relatives.

The process of distributing money orders once they reach
Western Samoa is fascinating because, unlike the more
private and straightforward cash-transfer and bank-
transfer processes, receipt of a money order is a public
affair. Almost nightly broadcasts of money-order recipients come over the radio, announcing the names and
villages of the recipients, who travel to the nearest
post office to pick up the money orders. In many cases,
the recipients are already aware that they will be receiving the money orders because their overseas relatives
or friends have notified them in advance by letter. The
broadcasts thus serve to summon those who have not been
notified and to brace recipients for the usual requests
for gifts, donations, loans, or repayment of credit.
Even though the amount is never announced on the radio,
it is not surprising that strategies for avoiding the
broadcast of names have developed.

The limited number of conversion centers draws a fairly
steady traffic of recipients all year around, although
the money-order trade is most striking just before
Christmas, when hundreds of people wait in long lines
at the post office in Apia for their remittances.
Villagers are at some disadvantage in this traffic,
for it takes them the longest to get to town, and it
costs them the most in terms of their round-trip bus fare.
Once the village recipient is in town, he or she may
spend part of the remittance on the less-expensive and
more varied goods of the port town. In addition, of
course, a trip to town provides the opportunity to visit
with relatives who may help with the bus fare or a small
gift. Recipients in Apia occasionally remark that their
rural relations receive larger money orders than they do
in order to help cover transportation costs. This idea
is supported to some extent by an examination of the
average value of money orders for nine villages, two
within the Apia area and seven located in rural Western
Samoa. The average for the two urban-area villages was
$WS 23.10, while for the seven rural villages the average
was $WS 25.70. This difference would be more than enough
to pay for the round trip from village to town.

Assuming that the distribution of all personal remittances
parallels the distribution of money orders (and there
is reason to believe that they do), a rough estimation
of remittance incomes as a percentage of total incomes
can be made. In 1969, net monitored and unmonitored
remittances averaged $WS 9.21 per capita and were dis-
tributed as follows:

TABLE 7:

ESTIMATED DISTRIBUTION OF REMITTANCE INCOME
BY AREA, 1969

	Estimated per capita remittance income ($WS)	Estimate of remittances as percentage of total income*
Apia area	23.21	22-28%
Upolu (outside Apia area)	7.14	20-26%
Savaii	3.32	7-10%

*Based on variable estimates of total income.

These estimates suggest that, although incomes are higher
in and around the port town of Apia, remittances supply
more cash, absolutely and proportionally, to the town
than they do to the rural areas. Since most migrants
come from the island of Upolu, and specifically from
the Apia area, the concentration of remittances in these
areas is predictable.

IMPACT OF REMITTANCES

The short-term, cash *impact* of remittances on Apia and
the rural areas is not as clear as remittance-distribution
data might indicate. The Apia area, containing 20% of
the population, receives almost 50% of all remittances,
while the 80% of the population in the villages receives
the remainder. Yet, because incomes are much lower in
the villages, remittances as a percentage of total income

for the many villages is often equal to or greater than
remittances as a percentage of total income in Apia.
Table 8 presents data on income components for several
villages ranked according to degree of isolation from
Apia. Even the most isolated villages (Sa'asi, Salani,
Taga, and Uafato) receive substantial income from
remittances.

Another factor to consider in assessing the differential
impact of remittances on town and village populations
is monetization. While the Apia area is almost fully
monetized, many villages are still in the process of
shifting from a localized "sphere-of-exchange" economy,
using indigenous media of exchange, to a nonlocalized
economy employing a generalized medium of exchange--money
(see Salisbury 1962; Nash 1966; Barth 1967b; Lockwood
1971). In those rural areas where monetization is still
underway, where incomes are low, and where income sources
are limited, remittances are a potentially important
means of speeding monetization, increasing income, and
broadening the sources of income.

Apart from monetization, there are structural factors
that influence the impact of remittances on the islands.
In both town and village, remittances are generally regarded as income supplements rather than income
substitutes because they are sent in amounts neither
sufficiently large nor sufficiently regular to replace
income from agriculture or wage labor. As income supplements, remittances may be used to cover normal expenses
or may be disbursed in consumption activities or through
redistribution. The use of remittances reflects the
relative economic position of different groups in the
islands' economy.

The two major groups of remittance recipients--part-Samoans
(also know as part-Europeans) and full-blooded Samoans--
have different constraints operating on their spending
patterns. For part-Samoans, with their higher standard
of living and easier access to capital and to employment
opportunities, remittances have less of an impact on
overall income. At the same time, because part-Samoans
do not fully participate in the many wealth-leveling
and redistributive activities that are so much a part
of Samoan village life, they have more options in terms
of conspicuous consumption and investment. For full-
blooded Samoans, lower incomes and greater obligations
to kin set certain limits on spending patterns. Samoan
remittance recipients are participants in an indigenous

44

TABLE 8:

VILLAGE INCOME COMPONENTS

Village	Percent of per capita income from agriculture	Percent of per capita income from wage labor	Percent of per capita income from remittances	Percent of per capita income from other sources	Source
Apia	--	78	16	6	Pitt 1970:273
Malie	29	43	12	16	Pitt 1970:273
Utuali'i	44	30	26	--	Lockwood 1971:350
Poutasi	55	31	14	--	Lockwood 1971:293
Sa'asi	37	2.5	58	2.5	Shankman
Salani	62	11	18	9	Pitt 1970:273
Taga	68	8	20	4	Lockwood 1971:227
Uafato	55	16	13	16	Lockwood 1971:146

45

status system in which mutual cooperation between kin is necessary to secure rank, prestige, and dignity. The resultant pooling of resources, including remittances, acts both to concentrate and to disburse wealth, but, given the structure of the Western Samoan economy, most of these funds are restricted to expenditures *within* the Samoan status system rather than serving as capital that can be used for upward mobility in the wider society.

As mentioned earlier, the Western Samoan economy is controlled by a small group of Europeans and part-Samoans. The amount of capital necessary to become competitive with businesses owned and operated by this segment is beyond the means of most Samoans, who are relegated to smaller and less profitable ventures. Anthropologist David Pitt has provided a comprehensive account of the consequences of European and part-Samoan economic dominance. He states that

> the most important reasons for failure or low profits [by Samoans] result from the monopolistic position of the big firms in Apia who ultimately control the buying and selling of most goods and many services... The big firms are able to perpetuate this monopoly by excluding Samoans from the European social group. This social group is an important reason, in fact, for the part-European and European success. (1970:259)

Furthermore, the economic elite, while encouraging consumption, discourages Samoan participation in the urban economy through certain discriminatory practices candidly referred to by Pitt:

> Many overseas Europeans and local part-Europeans tolerate a handful of high ranking Samoans or Samoans who stay 'in their place', i.e., in the village. But they intensely dislike and actively discriminate against Samoans and other Polynesians or Melanesians who aspire to urban residence. There is little the Europeans can do to stop Samoans acquiring the outward signs and symbols of European life if the Samoans have the money to purchase goods. But Europeans can, and do, restrict other forms of communication. (1970:184)

Lack of access to European and part-European social and economic circles is complicated by the customary system

46

of Samoan land tenure, which was formalized under the
German regime and codified into law during the New
Zealand mandate. Under this system, 80% of Western
Samoa's land belongs to Samoans, but because of legal
restrictions on individual ownership and the corresponding lack of secure tenure, Samoan land cannot
become competitive with plantation land owned by
Europeans and part-Europeans. In this way, the Samoan
communal land-tenure system contributes to an environment of limited Samoan opportunities.

Samoans are further constrained by the nature of credit
available to them. Small-time traders offer Samoans
credit at high interest rates. As Pitt explains:

> Many of these traders and money-lenders are
> considered credit-worthy by the trading bank
> and are able to borrow money at around 6 per
> cent interest rate, which is promptly lent to
> Samoans at interest rates of between 15 and
> 80 per cent. Again many Samoans, especially
> those dependent upon a fluctuating cash crop
> income, are forced to pledge their season's
> crops to traders and storekeepers at even
> higher interest rates. The result of this
> credit dependence on high interest, unofficial
> sources is indebtedness, defaulting, and
> possibly the origin of the myth that Samoans
> are not credit-worthy. (1970:211)

Remittances have provided Samoans with one means of
bypassing these illicit high-interest schemes, but
often remittances are used to pay off credit from the
trader and as a means of acquiring extensions on credit.
Samoan capital formation is also discouraged by credit
practices that favor consumption activities rather than
capital investment. Pitt notes:

> The traders, or at least the back-street or
> village traders who always give credit, con-
> centrate on the sale of consumer luxuries.
> Much capital equipment, especially the more
> expensive technological capital, can only be
> acquired from larger merchants or the Government
> who are very much more reluctant to give credit...
> Many Samoans feel that if capital formation
> is not possible, any savings should be used
> directly to secure status through ceremonial
> disbursement. "If I cannot get a ladder to

47

> pick all the bread-fruit on the tree, I will
> stand and pluck the lower branches,' as one
> chief put it. (1970:211-212)

Samoans are thus effectively excluded from large-scale,
capital-intensive ventures while being encouraged to
seek status in the Samoan sector.

It is clear from Pitt's discussion of the Samoan economic
niche within the Western Samoan economy that the con-
tinuation of pervasive wealth-leveling mechanisms such
as ceremonial redistribution and small-scale luxury
consumption are closely related to a lack of economic
options. Conspicuous giving and redistribution are
positively sanctioned and, when it is known that cash
is available, relatives will come to request gifts or
loans for church collections, weddings, feasts, funerals,
and other similar activities. These requests are difficult to refuse, and they must generally be met for the
maintenance of rank, prestige, and dignity within the
indigenous status system. Dispersal of remittances and
other cash income, as well as dispersal of consumer
goods, is not necessarily wasteful given the context in
which it occurs. As Tiffany (1975) points out, receiving
wealth entails giving it later on and, in the redistributive process, cash and goods are constantly flowing
back and forth. More importantly, redistribution allows
Samoans to obtain some measure of prestige and influence
in a system that virtually precludes their participation
at its highest levels. Although Samoans may wish for
more mobility within the Western Samoan economy, their
efforts are usually restricted to redistribution and
consumption of inexpensive imports, such as tinned
corned beef, canned fish, butter, sugar, tobacco,
clothing, and housing materials. For Samoans, then,
remittances have not generally provided access to
European and part-European economic circles, although
they have allowed some mobility within the Samoan sector.

The economic position of most Samoans in the Western
Samoan economy can be contrasted with a group receiving
remittances but who are not bound by institutional constraints. For part-Samoans and non-Samoan islanders,
the absence of institutional constraints means that remittances are more likely to be used for capital investment
or, if they are used for consumption, the amounts spent
will be larger since the remittances need not be redistributed. It is this group that is more likely to purchase
expensive consumer goods such as cars, motorcycles, and
European-style houses. Since this group is better off to

48

begin with, it is not surprising that they are in a better position to conspicuously consume or to invest. An example of one such upwardly mobile remittance recipient is Lotu, a non-Samoan islander who moved to Western Samoa with his parents as a youth. Although Lotu had a civil service job, his main form of income was remittances--over $WS 500 in 1969. These remittances came from contacts in another island group still under New Zealand mandate. Migrants from this island group pass through Western Samoa on their way to New Zealand and stay with Lotu and his family, who then receive a subsidy for the migrants' room and board from the New Zealand Government; in 1969, Lotu's family made $WS 70 by housing migrants. Most of the migrants are not closely related to Lotu, but by befriending them Lotu may receive a token remittance as a gift once the migrants reach New Zealand. Because the migrants have no claims on Lotu and because he is not part of the Samoan social system, Lotu may then spend the remittances as he chooses.

In 1969, after several years of increasing affluence due to remittances, Lotu decided to invest his money in a car to be used as a taxi. By hiring a driver, Lotu expected to augment his remittance and civil service incomes by $WS 200 a month in the lucrative taxi business. To purchase the car, Lotu took out a bank loan and a loan from a credit union, going over $WS 1500 into debt. The car itself was a fully equipped large Japanese sedan that cost a staggering $WS 2700. Unfortunately, the driver that Lotu had hired to drive this prestigious taxi was not earning what Lotu had expected, not even enough to pay off the loans, so Lotu took a leave of absence from his civil service post and drove the taxi himself. In a period of three months, Lotu had three accidents and the time-consuming taxi business was beginning to wear on him. His income did increase, though, and he was able to pay off the loans. Shortly thereafter, he gave up his car and his civil service post, and he began working for the Catholic church for a lower wage. Nonetheless, Lotu's remittances continued to enable him to lead a comfortable life by Samoan standards.

Although Lotu was not wealthy, he was well-to-do by Samoan standards, and he was able to engage in entrepreneurial activities because he was not limited by low income and by the leveling mechanisms of Samoan society. Relatively wealthy families have even more latitude in consumption activities. In wealthy families, the sending or bringing of remittances can actually be considered an

insult since it would imply that the family actually
needs money. Migrants from such families therefore
send little, saving their money to spend as they desire.
An example of one such migrant from a wealthy family is
Vi'i, the daughter of a prosperous trader. Vi'i attended
a Catholic school, learning English and secretarial
skills. At age 20, she left for New Zealand for two
years to work as a secretary. In 1969, she returned to
the islands to attend her sister's lavish European-style
wedding, using some of her savings to buy dresses for
bridesmaids at a cost of $WS 100. Vi'i had never sent
any money to her family and was adamant that the sending
of remittances would reflect poorly on her family. Her
return to Western Samoa was a short one; Vi'i found Apia
dull and confining compared to life in Auckland.

Most of the Samoan families do not have the options open
to part-Samoans or non-Samoan islanders such as Vi'i
and Lotu. Since remittances cannot be used by Samoans
for large-scale capital formation or expensive consumer
goods, Samoans use them for status activities and small-
scale consumption. Remittances are also reinvested in
migration because Samoans know that remittances sent or
brought back will more than offset the costs of migration,
will increase their purchasing power (Lockwood 1971:
203-206), and will make further migration possible,
thereby circumventing the limited opportunities in
Western Samoa. Referring to his reasons for migrating,
one civil servant put it this way:

> With the small amount of money we get from the
> government, we can't do the things we want for
> ourselves or for our children. So we try to
> find another way to make money.

By promoting migration and its many related activities,
by providing money for parents to educate their children
so that they, too, will be able to migrate, and by providing supplementary income to people in a deteriorating
economy, remittances symbolize the predicament of many
Samoans and provide a partial solution to it.

4   A Village and Its Remittances

Thus far, a general overview of migration, remittances, and underdevelopment in Western Samoa has been presented. To gain a clearer perspective on the effects of migration and remittances, this chapter offers a sketch of Sa'asi (a pseudonym), a small village of about 280 people located on the southern coast of Upolu, a few hours from Apia. In 1969, Sa'asi was the most remittance-dependent village in rural Western Samoa, with over half of its income derived from migrant remitters. It therefore provides some insight into the remittance situation that was to become more prevalent throughout rural Western Samoa in the 1970s.

THE VILLAGE SETTING

Sa'asi, like all Samoan villages, is composed of kinship units called '*āiga*. Although '*āiga* is sometimes translated as "extended family," an '*āiga* is actually a localized segment of a dispersed cognatic descent group, and each segment may contain more than one extended family. In Sa'asi, there are 17 '*āiga*, several containing two and three extended families. Membership in an '*āiga* provides the individuals and families within it access to land and social status, and so it is an important economic and political unit as well as a kinship unit. Yet membership in an '*āiga* is not fixed. Because descent is traced in a nonunilineal manner, an individual can belong to several '*āiga* whose members live in many parts of the islands. As Tiffany notes:

> Membership in an '*āiga* is optative, and not all potential '*āiga* memberships are activated and maintained. Indeed, it would be most difficult,

51

if not impossible, for an individual to meet the
political, economic, and psychological obligations
involved in maintaining active memberships in all
'āiga to which he could conceivably claim con-
sanguinity... The presence of multiple 'āiga
memberships in the Samoan system of nonunilineal
descent means that some members of an 'āiga will
be geographically dispersed, while other members
who choose to reside on that 'āiga's land will
constitute the localized core, or nucleus. Most
'āiga in Western Samoa are traditionally associated
with one particular village where the descent
group was believed to have its founder. Hence,
the localized residential core of an 'āiga occupies
the land which belongs to that 'āiga.... (1974:36)

Members of the 'āiga therefore maintain membership by
active participation in its activities.[1]

Within the village, each 'āiga has its own leader or
matai (sometimes translated as "chief") who is responsible
for the management of 'āiga land and affairs, including
the authority, honor, and dignity associated with each
'āiga title. Land and titles are the communal property
of the 'āiga and each 'āiga elects a matai or titleholder
who not only has 'āiga responsibilities, but also responsibilities within the village council and within the
larger indigenous Samoan status system. The 'āiga titles
are specifically ranked with respect to each other within
the village and throughout the islands, so that 'āiga
membership is an important indicator of social prestige.
It is expected that 'āiga members will help to maintain
this prestige by providing the proper service to their
matai. In turn, the matai is expected to manage 'āiga
land and labor within the village to insure his kin's
welfare. Each titleholder also represents his 'āiga in
the weekly meeting of the village council to legislate
village policy. The council, like the individual
titleholder, coordinates and regulates land and labor
usage with an emphasis on articulating production with
local needs and prestige activities.

---

[1]Samoan social structure is so complex and intricate
that this presentation cannot pretend to do ethnographic
justice to it. Fortunately, a number of fine studies
exist that the reader may consult for a more thorough
coverage. Many of these studies are listed in the
bibliography.

The basis of the village economic system is the control
of access to land and the regulation of the agricultural
labor force by individual titleholders and by the
village council. Communal control of land and titles
are codified into law and legitimized by the Western
Samoan state, but the system is ultimately dependent on
agriculture as the mainstay of the rural economy. Should
the economic basis of rural Samoan life change and agricultural production be reduced in significance, then
access to land and regulation of the labor force would
become less important; *'āiga* economic cooperation,
communal labor, and authority patterns would also change.
In essence, this is what has happened in Sa'asi in the
relatively brief period between 1950 and 1973. The
agricultural economy of the village has been undermined
by a number of factors, including migration and remittances. The dynamics of this process are reflected in
Sa'asi's economic history.

Although classified as a "traditional" Samoan village by
some observers, Sa'asi has been integrated into the
colonial and postcolonial political economy for the
past 90 years. Cash cropping, for example, was
established in the late nineteenth century. Although
Sa'asi's geographic isolation left the village oriented
primarily toward subsistence, cash cropping increased
as a series of stores was set up in the village by
traders representing the large European-owned merchant
firms in Apia. These stores stimulated production by
granting credit to be repaid in copra, thus incorporating
the villagers into the wider economy as small-scale con-
sumers and as producers for the export market. Yet the
village was small, with less than 200 people until the
1950s, and because of poor market linkage, copra production was limited. Sa'asi was, nevertheless, in a
favorable position to expand cash cropping once
transportation to the Apia market was improved. The
village occupied a sizeable and underused tract of land
with comparatively large family plots. Furthermore,
crops were cultivated separately rather than together
as they are in more densely settled villages (Farrell
and Ward 1962:187). Thus agricultural expansion could
include intercultivation as well as the cultivation of
unexploited plots of land.

In 1955, a road linking Sa'asi to the market in Apia
was completed, and villagers began to take advantage of
the potential for cash-crop expansion. Several other
changes in the 1950s accompanied expansion in copra production. In 1952, the lucrative banana crop was

introduced into the village. Bananas were relatively
easy to grow, and the government, rather than the village
trader, controlled banana marketing, buying directly
from the producers. The new income from bananas greatly
increased agricultural income. There was also a government program to encourage village producers to build
their own hot-air copra driers. Village traders had
always held a monopoly on copra marketing and, to a
large extent, on the processing of copra in hot-air
driers. Since this kind of processing yields the
highest-quality and highest-priced copra, villagers
with their own hot-air driers could receive higher
prices for their efforts. About two-thirds of the
families in Sa'asi proceeded to build the driers. The
road, the banana scheme, and the hot-air driers all
helped to increase income in the village; high prices
on the world market also helped, as these were reflected
in the prices paid to producers. Some villagers speak
glowingly of an era in the late 1950s and early 1960s
when they could make $WS 100 a month from agriculture.
Unfortunately, the boom was short-lived, and new
adaptations followed changing economic conditions.

By the early 1960s, production had begun to decline.
The coconut plantations were aging, and the trees were
yielding perhaps 20% fewer nuts. The remaining nuts
were decimated by coconut beetles and rats. In 1964,
bunchy-top virus reached Sa'asi's banana plantations
with disastrous effects. By 1969, there was no commercial
banana crop, which literally halved agricultural income.
Cocoa production, never a large part of the village's
cash-cropping efforts, was confined to domestic consumption in 1969. In the interim, some families had
turned to fishing and to taro, annatto, and tobacco to
increase their declining incomes, but these supplements
could not compensate for losses in the two major crops.

The hurricane of 1966 hastened the decline of the coconut
plantations, and the quality of copra was lowered due to
the altered credit policies of the one remaining trader.
Under the old credit policy, transactions with the
trader were collective, with the head of the *'āiga*
usually receiving payment and arranging credit terms
for the entire unit. The new policy provided credit
for payments to individuals, allegedly to increase
village purchasing power which had waned with the
attrition of the banana crop. The consequences of this
policy, however, were not beneficial to the villagers.
The immediate return on unprocessed nuts led individuals,
especially children, to climb the coconut trees and

collect the green nuts rather than waiting for them to
mature and fall. The unprocessed young nuts would then
be sold to the trader at half the value of hot-air-dried
copra and the trader would process them himself. This
fragmentation of cooperative production led most
families to abandon their own hot-air driers and to
rely on the trader's drier. The premature culling of
nuts led to a shortage in the supply of mature nuts and
to a lower quality of copra, the price of which continued
to drop as the use of young nuts relative to mature
nuts increased. The poor quality of copra led to
government action to prevent still further deterioration
of this situation, which was widespread in villages
throughout Western Samoa.

There were other changes in Sa'asi besides the agricultural
decline, especially after the hurricane of 1966. The
destruction wrought by the hurricane included many of
the houses in the village and, instead of rebuilding on
old housesites, many '*āiga* elected to move inland,
nearer to the road. The reasons for the move were
varied. Some '*āiga* complained of pigs uprooting crops
near the old housesites, of declining soil fertility,
and of theft in the village, while others wanted to be
closer to their plantations inland; factionalism within
one '*āiga* led one of the constituent families to re-
settle above the road. New branches of '*āiga* moving
into the village also chose to live near the road
rather than in the old village. Piped water helped to
make this dispersal possible; previously, a communal,
centralized, natural water supply had served the entire
village. This new combination of circumstances led to
the alteration of Sa'asi's geographic and spatial
cohesion.

The agricultural decline itself was not sufficient to
alter the village's social and political cohesion, because
fluctuations in production and income did not alter the
fundamental dependence on agriculture. Access to land
and regulation of the labor force continued to fall under
the jurisdiction of the '*āiga*, the *matai*, and the village
council. In the late 1950s and 1960s, however, a new
set of opportunities in wage labor opened up outside
the village. These opportunities--in Apia, American
Samoa, and New Zealand--offered a remunerative alternative to agriculture. Wage labor, usually acquired
through kin ties, was especially attractive to the
young adults in the village. The reasons for this
attraction were varied, but among them were a chance
for security apart from the '*āiga*, a means of meeting

'*āiga* obligations without the pressure of being in the village, the excitement of town, and the encouragement of relatives both in town and inside of the village.

A closer look at the village setting provides some context for the reasons behind the migration of the young adults. Given the communal nature of the land system and the nature of decision-making within the '*āiga* and the village, young adults sometimes found themselves bearing the burden of '*āiga* obligations with little input into the decision-making process. Furthermore, the rewards for service to the titleholder and the '*āiga* were often delayed and uncertain. Ultimately, it was expected that as young men grew older, they would receive titles of their own; in Sa'asi this usually took place after 40. There was no guarantee, though, that even the son of a titleholder would receive a title, since election to a title is the affair of all branches of the '*āiga*, the local core and dispersed membership. The insecurity of election to a prestigious title is further complicated by the lack of exclusive tenure under the system of communal land ownership. Under this system, land cannot be worked in an entrepreneurial fashion without consultation with the wider '*āiga*, nor can it be transferred directly from father to son. Such insecurities in village life made young men likely candidates for a more secure life in wage labor elsewhere. Occasionally, a young man dissatisfied with village life might leave the '*āiga* altogether since membership is optative, but this is easier said than done. An alternative is to use the '*āiga* as a means of migration. By migrating under the auspices of kin in the '*āiga* located in Apia, American Samoa, or New Zealand, young men and women remain within the '*āiga* and can fulfill their obligations without the immediate pressures and uncertainties of village life. By sponsoring and encouraging migration, the '*āiga* is able to derive some benefits, including remittances.

Titleholders often encouraged their sons and daughters to migrate, hoping that migration would ease tensions at home and supply sufficient remittances to compensate for the loss of their labor and services. Most of the titleholders were too old to participate in wage-labor migration themselves, although the few young titleholders in the village did move to Apia and New Zealand to take advantage of the new opportunities. As a group, the titleholders had no means of regulating migration; it was not within the scope of problems considered by the village council. The lack of consensus and the inability

56

to regulate a nonagricultural labor force led titleholders
to pursue diverse strategies. In the 1960s, some titleholders encouraged their immediate kin to migrate and
remit. Smaller *'āiga* would then invite poorer relatives
from other villages to move to Sa'asi in order to replace
lost manpower; these relatives were lured to the village
partly as a result of *'āiga* prosperity made possible by
the remitters and partly as a result of the promise by
the titleholder that they would be allowed some freedom
while still rendering certain valuable services. Still
other *'āiga* were unable to manipulate migration, remittances, and manpower to their advantage due to the
advanced age of their titleholders. These older titleholders had taken office following the great influenza
epidemic of 1918-1919, and they did not comprehend the
individuation of economic opportunity that was taking
place. While nominally in control of *'āiga* affairs,
actual decisions were now being made by younger, untitled
members.

As *'āiga* pursued different strategies to cope with the
new economic situation presented by wage-labor opportunities, the social and political cohesion of the *'āiga*
began to fragment. Cooperation and sharing within the
'āiga, formerly based on collective interest, were
modified by migration, changing economic fortune, and
the individuation of economic activity. Although the
number of *'āiga* in Sa'asi remained constant since the
1950s, the composition of the *'āiga* changed. By 1969,
some of *'āiga* had split, forming new, semiautonomous
family units within the village; that year, there were
26 such economic units within the village, often
operating without the leadership of a titleholder. The
economic fragmentation of *'āiga* was mirrored in conflicts
within and between *'āiga* over land and property, and
the village council found itself less able to success-
fully arbitrate these disputes. In 1969, the council
could not resolve a record high of five land cases which
then had to be referred to the national Land and Titles
Court.

MIGRATION AND REMITTANCES

Wage-labor migration played an important role in the
changing economic, political, and social life of Sa'asi.
The motivations for migration were undoubtedly more
complex than have been presented here, but the *pattern*
of migration in the late 1950s and 1960s clearly indicates the primacy of economic factors. Neither wage labor

nor migration alone could have produced the effects experienced in Sa'asi, but the combination of migration and wage labor, particularly permanent wage labor in New Zealand, was decisive.

In terms of the village's history, this pattern of migration was new, although migration itself had always been a part of village life. Villagers had never been confined to Sa'asi, and long before roads circled the island of Upolu, there were regular visitations between kin and political allies, including those as far away as American Samoa. Two residents of Sa'asi had even been to New Guinea as Christian missionaries at the turn of the century. When tighter communications and easier access to Apia were established during World War II, some of the villagers went to Apia and New Zealand to trade and to work in the war effort. Following World War II, visits to the port town and overseas increased. Some of Sa'asi's children went to school in Apia and later moved there or to other nearby villages to take civil service posts that they qualified for as a result of their education. Marriage drew still other villagers away from Sa'asi, and by the 1960s, daily bus service to Apia stimulated further travel.

Whatever the earlier reasons for migration, kin in town and overseas began to provide connections to wage-labor opportunities. The deteriorating agricultural situation and the remittances sent or brought back helped to reinforce the pattern of wage-labor migration through kin auspices and, by the 1960s, relatives in New Zealand had become the most important link in the chain of migration and remittance dependence. The predominant pattern of migration was one in which rural villagers had left the village permanently to live almost 1,600 miles away in Auckland.

Most of Sa'asi's migrants resided in New Zealand on a permanent basis. Of 45 active remitters permanently abroad in 1969, there were 37 in New Zealand, but only 6 were in American Samoa and 2 were in the United States. The remittances of these permanent New Zealand migrants coupled with those of migrants temporarily in New Zealand were the major source of income for the village. In 1969, remittances comprised 58% of Sa'asi's total cash income, with 82% of the remittances coming from New Zealand. Most, but not all, of the migrants remitted, and in 1969 there were a number of migrants living permanently in New Zealand who sent nothing. Generally speaking, these were migrants who had lived abroad for several years and would send money on request, but not on a regular basis. All active remitters were close kin, usually sons or daughters of older village residents, or older people themselves paying a visit to their children. The active remitters fell into three broad categories: (1) migrants residing permanently overseas in New Zealand, American Samoa, or the United States; (2) village members temporarily overseas; and (3) village members residing in other parts of Western Samoa. The following table indicates the amount of money sent by each category of remitter:

TABLE 9:

AMOUNT REMITTED BY RESIDENCE OF REMITTERS, 1969

	Number	Male	Female	Amount ($WS)
Remitters permanently overseas	45	17	28	3907.*
Remitters temporarily overseas	11	7	4	2089.
Remitters residing in other parts of Western Samoa	11	9	2	438.
Totals	67	33	34	6434.

*Plus 7 fares to New Zealand.

Migrants permanently overseas in New Zealand accounted for most of Sa'asi's remittances, both directly and indirectly. In addition to sending and bringing remittances, these permanent migrants were expected to facilitate and finance the migration of other 'āiga members, often providing relatives with travel fares, housing, food, pocket money, and job connections. Relatives temporarily in New Zealand were then able to remit more, precisely because the bulk of their expenses was underwritten by permanent migrants. Sa'asi's temporary migrants comprised only 16% of the village's remitters, but supplied almost one-third of all remittances due to the assistance of their overseas sponsors.

59

There was another reason why temporary migrants tended
to remit more--their temporary visas made their return
to the village imminent, and it was important to bring
as much money home as feasible since its redistribution
reflected on the prestige and the economic status of
the 'āiga. Although many of these temporary migrants
would return to New Zealand, the immediacy of kin
pressures within the village required visiting members
to participate in redistributive activities. These
pressures applied to both temporary migrants and
visiting permanent migrants. Under such circumstances,
it was not surprising that the largest remittances were
brought in person rather than sent through the mails.
In 1969, the largest remittances were brought by two
young men who had worked for a short time in Auckland;
each returned with about $WS 700. The next largest
remittance was $WS 500 brought by three sisters who
had pooled their money to return for their father's
funeral in the village. After a brief sojourn, they
returned to their permanent homes in Auckland.

Apart from major events such as funerals, weddings, and
church openings, migrants permanently overseas were
under less pressure to remit or otherwise participate
in village activities than temporary migrants and
migrants residing in other parts of Western Samoa.
The fact of secure employment in New Zealand, or at
worst, adequate welfare, has led permanent migrants to
become less oriented to village life and less committed
to returning to it. They are prepared to fulfill their
'āiga obligations, but distance and relative wealth
in New Zealand have made village commitments less
intense. This may help to explain why the longer a
migrant is in New Zealand, the less likely he or she
is to send remittances on a regular basis, although
most permanent migrants do send small money orders on
an infrequent basis. Unless specifically requested,
these money orders are not earmarked for any particular
purpose. Such remittances serve as a token investment
in the future should the migrants return to Sa'asi for
a visit. They not only help kin financially, but also
promote good will and preserve good faith in circumstances where family ties could otherwise be minimized.

Women were the most reliable remitters, and young
unmarried women were encouraged to migrate because
they would honor their close kin ties with remittances.
The motivations behind the migration of these young
women were somewhat different than those for young men,

60

and as a result, the influence of the *'āiga* was stronger for women than men. Although the sex ratio of Sa'asi's migrants was fairly balanced, among active remitters, women outnumbered men and tended to send more money. Table 10 documents this point for remitters living permanently in New Zealand.

TABLE 10:

AMOUNT REMITTED BY MIGRANTS RESIDING PERMANENTLY
IN NEW ZEALAND TO SA'ASI BY SEX OF REMITTER, 1969
(n=37)

	Less than $WS 50	$WS 50 to $WS 99	$WS 100 to $WS 199	More than $WS 200	Number of remitters
Male	9	1	3	2	15
Female	8	4	6	4	22

Because women supply most of Sa'asi's remittances and because women receive over 40% of the money orders themselves, thus controlling their expenditure, the women of Sa'asi have much more economic leverage than they did before migration became important. It is sometimes thought that women are more responsible with money, and the alleged irresponsibility of men is cited as a reason for women receiving a high proportion of the remittances. When men go to town to cash money orders, they are said to squander it on minor pleasures, but, as common as this argument is, it is not entirely accurate. The men of the village are, for the most part, as careful with their money as the women. If the men were so improvident, an even higher proportion of money orders should be expected to go directly to women. In fact, female remitters send money to both sexes, depending at least as much on the occasion as on potentially irresponsible handling of the money.

REMITTANCE INCOME, CAPITAL, AND VILLAGE INSTITUTIONS

Male and female remitters together helped to compensate for income lost during the agricultural decline. Table 11 shows that of the village's income components, remittances were the most important component in 1969.

61

TABLE 11:

ESTIMATED TOTAL INCOME OF SA'ASI BY COMPONENTS, 1969
(IN $WS)

Agricultural income		Subtotals:
Villagers (including fishing)	2550.	
Trader	1500.	
		4050.
Remittance income		
New Zealand money orders	2707.	
Other New Zealand receipts	2534.	
American Samoan and U.S. receipts	755.	
Local receipts	438.	
		6434.
Other income		
All other sources	740.	
		740.
Total	11,224.	11,224.

In 1969, the average per capita income in Western Samoa was about $WS 39, with rural per capita income running about $WS 23, largely from agriculture. Sa'asi's per capita income was $WS 39.94. In terms of rural villages, then, Sa'asi was well-to-do.

Within the village, '*āiga* income and family income within the '*āiga* were highly variable. Table 12 reveals that of Sa'asi's 26 semiautonomous family units, 7 families received no remittances. Some of these 7 families had been recipients in the past while others would become recipients in the future, but these nonreceivers were a small minority of the village's population; only 16% of Sa'asi's residents were nonreceivers. The other 19 families, comprising 84% of the population, were heavily dependent on remittances. For receiving families, remittances constituted almost 76% of their total cash income. Data from Table 12 indicate that among receiving families, there was considerable variability in income, but, with the exception of the trader, most remittance-receiving families were much better off than nonreceivers. If the trader's income were excluded, remittance receivers would have made much more on the average than nonreceivers; this does not include remitted commodities, which would have made the difference even greater. Remittances were the most important source of wealth differences within and between receiving and nonreceiving groups. These differences were evident between '*āiga* that were still economically intact and within certain '*āiga* that had fragmented. In such cases, it was not unusual to find one branch of the '*āiga* dependent on remittances while the other branch received none directly.

While remittances provided recipients with a higher standard of living than village agriculture alone would have, they were neither sufficiently large nor sufficiently regular to radically transform the village economy. Most remittances were not used for capital investment, or, to be more specific, for *speculative* capital investment (J.L. Watson 1975:158). That is, remittances and other cash income did not usually go into innovative, local, entrepreneurial ventures. Rather, they went into *security* investments, such as houses, small-scale luxury consumption, and redistribution within the Samoan status system, including church donations. Remittances were also used to promote migration, but there was little saving from remittances, and their use for agricultural projects was still in the planning stage. Three receiving families did have savings

63

TABLE 12:

ESTIMATED FAMILY INCOME BY COMPONENTS, SA'ASI, 1969
(IN $WS)

	Remittance income	Agricultural income	Other income	Total income
Remittance-receiving	1.	140.		141.
families (n=19)	12.	120.		132.
	30.	106.		136.
	38.	82.		120.
	84.	129.		213.
	108.	66.		174.
	110.	140.		250.
	157.	74.		231.
	163.	50.		213.
	185.	57.		242.
	223.	70.	80.	373.
	329.	20.		349.
	454.	30.		484.
	476.	93.		569.
	524.	324.		848.
	584.	50.		634.
	663.	4.		667.
	1132.	123.		1255.
	1161.	79.		1240.
	6434.	1757.	80.	8271.
Nonreceiving		120.		120.
families (n=7)		140.		140.
		30.		30.
		120.		120.
		263.		263.
		140.		140.
Trader		1500.	300.	1800.
		2293.	300.	2593.

Collective income   360.

Total village income   11,224.

Note: These estimates were calculated from a village economic
       census. The reliability of the data is discussed in
       the Appendix.

accounts, but even though remittances were a new source
of income not directly tied to the trader, remittances
did not function as speculative capital.

To understand why this conservative pattern of
remittance use persists, it is necessary to examine
the *relationship* between agriculture and remittances
and the *institutional matrix* through which remittances
pass in the village, i.e., the trader, the *'āiga*, and
the church. Although agricultural income and remittance income are listed as separate components in
Table 12, there is a close relationship between the
two, revolving around the role of the village trader,
Sa'asi's wealthiest individual in 1969. The trader
was a major point of articulation for all forms of
cash income, and his ability to use different types of
income to his advantage enabled him to adjust to the
agricultural decline while maintaining his monopoly
on trade and credit. The failure of remittances to
undermine the trader's position constituted one set
of limits on the transformation of the village economy.

As mentioned earlier, traders were formerly adjuncts
to the large import-export firms in town that had
established rural stores to stimulate production and
import demand through credit. Recently, these stores
have shifted to independent part-Samoan and Samoan
ownership, since the large firms no longer require
them as incentives, and because purchasing power is
great enough that the firms no longer need to take
credit risks (Pitt 1970:248). Sa'asi's trader is a
successful part-Samoan whose family has powerful commercial ties in villages throughout the region. As
the village's sole buyer of copra and sole importer
of goods, he has held a virtual monopoly on Sa'asi's
trade and credit since 1956. Some villagers have
occasionally sought credit in the stores of adjacent
villages and have done some trading there, but Sa'asi's
trader bought most of the village's copra. As the
volume of copra production dropped in the 1960s, the
trader changed his credit policy to compensate for
losses by granting individual credit and by accepting
low-quality nuts for processing. In doing so, he was
able to purchase more unprocessed nuts, thus making up
for lost volume through lower buying costs. Normally,
the lower prices paid to villagers for unprocessed
copra would have dampened import demand by lowering
purchasing power, and the trader's credit policy would
have been self-defeating. Remittances, however, have
increased village purchasing power, and the trader's

store now contains a wider variety of consumer goods than ever before. The potential for remittances has also allowed villagers to get further extensions of credit from the trader. Thus, in circumstances that might otherwise have weakened the trader's position, remittances have aided in maintaining his profits and his central role in the village economy.

If remittances have not substantially weakened the role of the trader, they have weakened the economic and political solidarity of the 'āiga. Some of the effects of remittances have already been dealt with, but it is the *process* of remittance redistribution that has led to these consequences. As a new form of income, remittances are not subject to the same kind of redistributive pressures within the 'āiga as other forms of income, for in remittance redistribution, the titleholder can be bypassed as the redistributive agent. As an example, in 1972, two nontitleholders returned from New Zealand with sums of $WS 700 and $WS 400. The nontitleholders controlled the distribution of their remittances, using some for the education of their children and for prestige foods as well as clothing, church donations, and a small portion for agricultural equipment. The remainder was redistributed to relatives over a period of weeks with the titleholder and married brothers and sisters getting most of the money. More remote 'āiga relations also received some money, but others received nothing. One such nonrecipient was quite bitter, calling his kinsman a "bloody bastard," although by this time the remitter had nothing left, even for himself. Nevertheless, the nonrecipient felt that if the distribution had been conducted by the titleholder, rather than one of the young men, he would have had a better chance of getting some of the money.

Samoans explain that such "selfishness" will lead to poverty, while prosperity and wealth come from sharing and redistribution (Pitt 1970:27). Certain migrants, however, especially those returning to the village, do not look forward to sharing with the wider 'āiga. Both remitters and recipients tend to regard remittances as personal property rather than 'āiga property and, despite sanctions for wider redistribution, the sharing of remittances has become more confined to the immediate family. Junior family members, both men and women, have wrested a certain degree of economic control from the titleholder as remittances have allowed families

66

some economic independence within the *'āiga*. This independence, while by no means complete, is recognizable and has led to inequalities within the *'āiga*.

Because titleholders often do not directly control the auspices of migration or the distribution of remittances, they must try to make the best of the situation by becoming remittance recipients and then generously redistributing the wealth. As a result, there is a paradoxical trend in which the titleholder can retain and even gain prestige through remittance distribution, while at the same time the ultimate basis of prestige is being diminished by migration and remittances. When the poorest family head in Sa'asi, a nontitleholder, can return from New Zealand with $WS 600 to redistribute, as he did in 1972, titleholders as individuals and as a group are reminded of the limitations on their own abilities as redistributive agents. While the titleholders still command considerable respect and influence, the purview of their influence seems to have waned. Communal labor projects that in the past were supervised by titleholders are on the decline, and even the process of election to a title can now be influenced by remittances.

Villagers were well aware of the importance of remittances to their welfare and prestige within the *'āiga*. This awareness was heightened by government radio broadcasts of the names of money-order recipients and by the fact that, until very recently, recipients had to travel to Apia to cash their money orders. The broadcasts have helped radio to become a very popular medium in Sa'asi. Radios purchased in town or brought back from overseas have increased in number from two in 1962 to 17 in 1969. Even if family members themselves did not receive money orders, radio broadcasts would inform them of *'āiga* members who had, in which case the recipients might be asked for money for special events, gifts, loans, or payment of debts. One ploy used to put off such requests by distant relations was to politely but unmistakably denounce the remitters as cheapskates who had sent only token remittances. This ploy, as with other means of avoiding the omnipresent wealth-leveling mechanisms in Samoan society, was only partially effective. In a small village, secrets were not well kept, and jealousies and tensions developed over the suspected hoarding of remittances. Accusations of hoarding were not uncommon, although remittances were often expended on items of value to the whole family or *'āiga*. One such expenditure was

housing materials, particularly metal roofs. Among
receiving families, all had metal roofs on at least one
house, while among nonreceivers only the trader and an
'āiga that had previously received remittances had
metal roofs. Prestige foods to be shared with relatives
were also of value to the group; these included canned
corned beef, canned fish, sugar, and butter, all available
from the trader. Such expenditures represent the security
investments referred to earlier.

Apart from the 'āiga and the trader, remittances also
passed through another village institution--the church.
In a normal year, church expenses for a family might
run between 10% and 25% of all cash income (see
Lockwood 1971:83), but in the 1960s, residents of
Sa'asi had found themselves being asked to contribute
larger amounts, culminating in the construction costs
of an elaborate new house for the Samoan pastor of the
village's dominant congregation.

On returning from New Zealand in 1970, the pastor of
the Christian Congregational Church decided to build
a lavish European-style house, complete with plumbing.
Although the pastor had brought back $WS 3000, the
largest remittance in the village's history, the estimated cost of the house was $WS 7000. Thus, donations,
or more appropriately, tithes, were requested from each
of the congregation's 24 member families and their
relatives in town and overseas.

In times of relative prosperity, the building of new
houses for clergy and new churches is commonplace
throughout Western Samoa. In Sa'asi, this particular
pastor had built a new and costly house only 6 years
earlier, in 1964. Such publicly supported works are
often cited as testimonials to the Samoan "love of
God," but there are other factors to consider when
assessing the means for financing these costly projects.
The pastor is a Samoan who does not hold a title. He
is, nonetheless, a central focus in competitive
status-seeking activities between 'āiga, blocks of
'āiga, and villages. Lockwood explains:

> The material support of the pastor (and his family)
> is often a fairly heavy charge on the village,
> particularly when the standard of upkeep becomes
> a subject of village pride and intervillage
> rivalry. Villages tend to compete with each
> other in the standard of housing provided for
> the pastor, in the impressiveness and size of

the church funds. Within the village, cash and
commodity 'gifts' to the pastor and church are
made publicly and by '*āiga* rather than by
individuals and this often becomes a matter of
inter-'*āiga* rivalry. (1971:34)

These rivalries are highlighted every Sunday in church,
when the names and amounts given by each '*āiga* are
publicly announced. Those '*āiga* who give too little
will suffer a loss of prestige, while those who give
the most may gain status. This simple mechanism, with
its power to shame or to honor, is an important incentive, inducing '*āiga* to support the church and the
pastor. The '*āiga* is thus an important unit from the
pastor's point of view, but not so important that the
pastor has been insensitive to the weakening of the
economic unity of a number of '*āiga*. To insure
continued support, tithes are now levied on an individual and family basis, as well as on the '*āiga*.

It is remarkable that, given the inducements to support
the church, some '*āiga* in Sa'asi were reluctant to
provide money for the pastor's new house. In light
of the years that it had taken to repay the costs of
the last house, resentment began to mount and,
eventually, it became so great that four titleholders,
including the church secretary, withdrew from the
congregation. These titleholders and their families
refused to donate any money to the church. While
other '*āiga* did donate appropriate sums, many members
were dissatisfied with the pastor, and their discontent
did not remain entirely latent. A story told in the
women's committee indicates some of the feeling about
the pastor. It seems, according to the storyteller,
that Jesus Christ returned to Samoa and attempted to
find his servant, the pastor. Christ went from hut to
hut without any luck and was about to leave when he
saw a large, fancy house. Passing by he remarked that
the pastor could not possibly live in such a house
because a pastor is a servant of God and would only
live in a humble dwelling.

Remittances provided an estimated three-quarters of the
money needed for the pastor's new house. Without remittances, most of the '*āiga* in the village could not
have met their tithes. A typical '*āiga* was asked to
contribute about $WS 10 a month for well over a year.
At the elaborate house opening, an additional sum of
money was expected, as well as four to seven fine mats

69

per *'āiga*; the fine mats alone are extremely valuable
and are difficult to obtain in quantity. To meet these
obligations, an extended kin network was summoned to
help shoulder a financial burden that could cost an
'āiga $WS 300. Since many *'āiga* in Sa'asi did not
make this much money in a year, special pressure was
put on remitters, especially those in New Zealand, to
enable families in the village to maintain their
prestige and dignity. At the house opening, some of
the money and many goods donated to the pastor were
redistributed to congregation members and their
relatives. This redistribution aided somewhat in
easing the large financial burden of the villagers.

The money for the pastor's house was handled through
a savings account in Apia and managed by a well-educated
district political figure who made direct purchases
on the account in town. The balance on the account
was then announced in church every Sunday. This
method of financing the house differed markedly from
the way money had been handled in the building of the
pastor's previous house. The first house had been
built on agricultural credit from the village trader
and with materials purchased through him. At that
time, the trader was the only individual who could
obtain money for such an undertaking. Church members
(who at that time included all of the villagers) were
then compelled to produce copra against the trader's
bill. Many people suspected the trader, who kept the
accounting to himself, of grossly overcharging, but
since literacy in the village was minimal, there was
no way of checking the trader's honesty. This time,
with an educated person handling the money and with
the trader bypassed in the financing of the house, people
were more trusting of the means if not the ends of
the house-building operation.

The completed house was monumental, a three-winged,
pastel-colored, plaster and cement domicile that is one
of the more garish structures in all of southern Upolu.
On completion, the pastor even put in a rug, which
immediately began rotting in the tropical climate.
His future plans included the purchase of Sa'asi's
first automobile, but it remained to be seen whether
church members would supply him the necessary funds.

From this consideration of the village institutional
matrix through which remittances pass, it is clear
that, as yet, remittances have not substantially
eroded the position of the church and its pastor, nor

70

have they altered the position of the trader. Migration
and remittances, however, have weakened the economic
and political position of the 'āiga, although this
effect has not been uniform for all Sa'asi's 'āiga.
Both the pastor and the trader are outside of the
Samoan status system and hence outside of the 'āiga;
they are therefore in a better position to take
advantage of the workings of the system in support of
their roles. Neither the pastor nor the trader has
direct control of access to land or the agricultural
force, as do the titleholders. Yet the trader supplies
cash, credit, and goods necessary for participation in
'āiga activities, while the pastor remains a central
focus of these activities. It seems quite possible
that, in a rural village setting, these non-Samoan
institutions can continue to thrive as the Samoan
'āiga system itself is modified.

Whatever the pattern of institutional change in the
future, the structures through which remittances
currently pass do not lead to speculative capital
formation for the villages. Money sent or brought,
or earned through cash cropping, is channeled through
the 'āiga and into the hands of the trader and the
pastor. With a fair proportion of the village's income
channeled to the trader and pastor, there is little
money remaining for investment. Even if there were
substantial sums of money available, the very structure
of the village economy would work against speculative
capital formation. Lack of local opportunities and the
generally low level of income, despite remittances,
have combined to promote migration activities as an
alternative to village life for younger people and as
a means of adequate support for those remaining behind.

Parents see migration as a way out of the village for
their children and sometimes themselves, and remittances
as affording a more comfortable life for those who do
not migrate. In strictly monetary terms, migration was
a far more lucrative investment than anything available
in the village, and a good deal of local expenditure
went into migration-related costs, such as visa arrangements, clothes, suitcases, trips back and forth to town,
farewell parties, transportation to the airport or
boat, fares, and pocket money. Often much of this
money was remitted by 'āiga members in New Zealand,
but for those without adequate funds, villagers
sometimes went to incredible lengths. One titleholder
surreptitiously attempted to sell a piece of his
family's land in order to get enough money to send

71

his daughter to New Zealand, a dubious practice under
Samoan law that was soon uncovered; the titleholder
was taken to court. Another man attempted to get for
his son, a known criminal and therefore ineligible for
migration, a New Zealand visa. The pastor "borrowed"
part of the village's $WS 200 bank loan for his fare
to New Zealand. This money, plus $WS 40 raised at a
village dance and also "borrowed" by the pastor, was
supposed to go into a village banana project. Most of
the families received enough money for migration
activities from their relatives overseas, but these
examples illustrate the importance of migration to
those who were otherwise unable to leave.

DEMOGRAPHIC EFFECTS AND AGRICULTURAL PRODUCTION

Migration has altered the demographic structure of the
village. The departure of many working-age males and
females has left Sa'asi with a majority of its population
under 15 years of age. If the population over 60 is
included, the dependent population would total 63% of
the village's residents. In comparative perspective,
this translates into a high dependency ratio (see
Dorjahn 1965:140), although not as high as in some
remittance-dependent areas such as the Caribbean
(Frucht 1966:149). Nevertheless, in 1969, most of
Sa'asi's residents were nonproducers, a point documented
by the village's age-sex structure in Table 13.

Migration over the last decade has caused an absolute
decrease in the 1961 baseline population, and new
families have replaced migrants at a rate sufficient
to keep the total population constant in the 1960s, as
Table 14 demonstrates. The heaviest attrition has been
in the working age groups. The 67 active remitters
living permanently or temporarily outside of the
village in 1969 would have constituted over one-third
of the village's labor force, and their loss has influenced agricultural production, although this
influence is neither as direct nor as obvious as
might be expected.

Townsmen and villagers alike remark that Sa'asi has had
more than its share of "laziness" and that remittances,
by providing an alternative source of income, have
acted as a disincentive to agriculture production.
After all, they argue, if a family can get enough
money to buy food and other goods through remittances,

72

TABLE 13:

AGE-SEX STRUCTURE OF SA'ASI, 1969

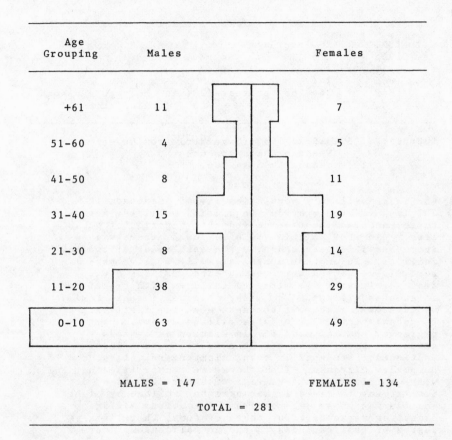

Age Grouping	Males	Females
+61	11	7
51-60	4	5
41-50	8	11
31-40	15	19
21-30	8	14
11-20	38	29
0-10	63	49

MALES = 147   FEMALES = 134

TOTAL = 281

TABLE 14:

POPULATION SIZE OF SA'ASI, 1951-1969

1951	200 estimate
1956	236
1961	278
1966	241
1969	265-285 for year (281 is the figure used in all calculations)*

Sources: 1956, 1961, 1966 (November) from Government of
          Western Samoa censuses.
          1969 census by Shankman.

*A Samoan village's population may vary between 10 and
20% in any given year due to spatial mobility, departures, and what must be called the "vagaries of human
life." In 1969, within a single month, there was an
increase of 19 people due to the settlement of two new
families. In another month, a family of five temporarily disbanded when the husband left for New
Zealand, leaving his wife and children with relatives
in another village. The older children in this family
would number eight but the next week the family might
be nonexistent in terms of a village census. The
degree of spatial mobility in Western Samoa causes
census problems because of the special cases just
mentioned: students in town, visiting relatives, and
temporary migrants. Then there are people like the
wife who lives in the village with her husband by day
but returns to sleep in her parents' village by night
and the man whose job keeps him in another village
except on weekends. For these reasons, there is a
degree of arbitrariness in the actual census figure.

---

why should family members have to engage in agriculture?
Despite its popularity, this argument is not an accurate
reflection of reality. First of all, among remittance-receiving families, remittances have not been
able to entirely replace agriculture as a source of
cash income nor have villagers been able to purchase
enough food with remittances to give up subsistence
activities.

A major portion of agricultural labor goes into
subsistence production, and since some subsistence
crops, such as coconuts and taro, can be used as cash
crops, there can be a trade-off between domestic consumption and cash cropping. When conditions require
increased domestic consumption or other noncash use of
these crops, remittances can be used to replace cash
losses. Lockwood notes this process of substitution
in the village of Utuali'i (1971:206). Yet the substitution of remittances for food and goods produced
through subsistence activities can go only so far under
conditions of limited income. Local foods at the Apia
market are expensive, while imported foods are luxuries
in town as well as in the village. Moreover, if relatives have to depend too heavily on other 'āiga members
for food, these kin may find their own cash-crop
earnings falling. For these reasons, all 'āiga in
Sa'asi and all families within the 'āiga continue subsistence activities. In addition, all families have
enough of a margin remaining for village activities
and for sale.

It is this necessity for *some* agricultural production
that allows 'āiga to maintain influence over their
members and thus remain a significant organizational
unit in the village despite the fragmenting forces of
migration and remittances. In the village, remittances can *supplement* but not *substitute* completely for
agricultural activities, especially in the subsistence
sphere, unless the remittances come in much larger sums
and at more regular internals. In discussing the
problem of substitution, one family head stated that
if she could not get relatives to work 'āiga land, she
would use her remittances to hire labor for subsistence
rather than be forced to purchase her family's food from
the store. Pitt notes that even wage laborers in Apia
do not make enough money for complete substitution, and
so they are "forced to make gardens for subsistence or
cash sales, or to rely on the generosity of others to
eke out their miserable stipends" (1970:171).

A second flaw in the argument that remittances produce
laziness stems from the actual money-earning potential
within the village. While it is true that families
with remitters would request money if they needed a
large sum quickly, this was not a result of laziness
so much as it was a realistic appraisal of their limited
cash-earning abilities under present agricultural conditions. For small amounts of money, villagers preferred
cash cropping, a loan from the trader, or borrowing from
local relatives, rather than sending requests for remittances from abroad. When small sums of money are needed,
it can be embarrassing for a titleholder to have to
request such a gift from a junior member of the *'āiga*.
On the other hand, if a large sum of money is needed
within a short space of time, remittances will be requested with the knowledge on the part of all concerned
that local sources are inadequate.

If remittances actually did act as a disincentive to
agricultural production, it should be expected that
agricultural incentives would carry little weight.
Yet in Sa'asi, most remittance-receiving families
responded actively to agricultural-production incentives. When shortages of taro and coconuts were
said to have led to theft within the village in 1969,
a taro-planting competition was held, with most of the
village's young men participating. The winner and
runner-up both came from remittance-receiving families.
The competition was sponsored by the pastor and some
remittance-receiving titleholders, who were also large
cash croppers (in village terms) and who were tired of
having to police their produce. A government-sponsored
coconut-planting project also met with a positive
response. Almost all remittance-receiving families
planted coconuts despite mixed feelings about the
government's program and despite the fact that many
did not receive the monetary incentive that was
promised to them.

Most villagers went to their plantations regularly to
cultivate and weed them. They regarded 1969 and the
previous five years as "bad," but they did not intend
to give up cash-crop production. The village as a
whole expected to return to banana cultivation in
1970 with the passing of the bunchy-top virus.
Collectively, Sa'asi had taken out a $WS 200 bank
loan in order to finance the undertaking, although
part of this sum subsequently was "borrowed" by the
pastor for migration. Smaller groups of individuals

also decided to enter into group banana ventures,
having witnessed successful replanting schemes in
neighboring villages.

While banana production did not increase as expected
in the next three years, the taro and coconut plantings
did help the village. The taro-planting competition
yielded food for domestic consumption and thus helped
curb theft; it also produced taro surpluses for sale at
the market in Apia and overseas, and so taro became a
cash crop. One consequence of the sale of taro was an
alternative source of cash-crop income. The cash earned
from taro enabled the villagers to allow the young
coconuts planted under the government program to mature.
The new coconuts on reaching maturity were able to re-
verse the previous decline in copra production to a point
where many families began to use their old hot-air
driers once again. Two other changes also stimulated
copra production: a reversal of the policy of allowing
individuals to sell green nuts to the trader and an
increasing number of people marketing their copra in
town rather than in the village. In 1970, the village
council prohibited individuals from selling immature
coconuts to the trader, thereby allowing the nuts to
ripen and eventually to be converted into top-grade
copra. This move helped the village to double its
copra production between 1970 and 1972, although
world prices for copra fluctuated, and income from
cash cropping increased only slightly. To get more
money for their copra, villagers began taking more of
their copra to Apia, where higher prices were paid.
Because remittances allowed people to purchase goods
without committing their copra as credit and because
transportation to town improved, villagers were able
to bypass the trader in this instance. The trader
also lost some income because villagers were using
their own hot-air driers.

There is some question, though, as to how far cash
cropping can expand, even under favorable conditions.
The theft that has plagued the village is still present
and tends to discourage some villagers from increasing
their plantings of taro and coconuts; low prices for
copra also discourage production; and the increasingly
dependent age structure of the village is leading to
greater subsistence consumption of garden produce
thus reducing the amount available for the market.
Sa'asi's newer residents have had a similar depressant
effect on cash-crop production. Of the four families
that have recently moved to the village, only 14 of

42 people could be classified as economically active, and their combined annual income from cash cropping was less than $WS 50. With no plantations of their own when they moved into Sa'asi, these new families were dependent on relatives whose own cash-cropping income was reduced by the need to feed the new arrivals. Since it takes several months at minimum before new plantations begin to yield taro and several years before coconuts begin to flourish, these new families were a continuing drain on their kin. Unlike the families that moved to Sa'asi in the early 1960s, however, these new families were heavily remittance dependent, receiving over $WS 550 in 1969. In another year, one family received over $WS 1000, most of it from a young man who had returned from New Zealand for a visit and was about to leave again. A second family received $WS 100 from a son who had just arrived in New Zealand. A third family who had just moved to the village received only a pig from local relatives, but they drew on the income from the titleholder with whom they were affiliated. The fourth family received about $WS 400 from relatives overseas. These new families were thus able to help their village sponsors offset possible cash-cropping losses through remittances.

The factors limiting the further expansion of cash cropping contribute to further migration. Sa'asi is rural and has minimal wage-labor opportunities. To raise income levels significantly, villagers must migrate. In 1969, all 26 families in the village expressed a desire to increase income. Many family members felt that in spite of remittances, they needed additional money to meet local obligations and to cope with the constantly rising prices of consumer goods. Lower-status titleholders and nonreceivers were particularly interested in migration as a means of improving their status and their standard of living. Of the seven nonreceiving families in 1969, four had become remittance recipients by 1973. Two of these families, the poorest in the village, had left Sa'asi by 1973, seeking better prospects with 'āiga members in other parts of Western Samoa.

SOCIAL CONSEQUENCES AND AN 'ĀIGA HISTORY

The impact of migration and remittances on family structure and residential cohesion has been substantial, but it does not always follow patterns observed

elsewhere in the world. Researchers in many remittance-
dependent areas, for example, have witnessed the breakdown
of the extended family and the rise of the consanguineal
family as a result of heavy migration (see Gonzales'
survey 1969). In their extreme form, these patterns
have not been observed in Sa'asi. The larger 'āiga unit
has been reduced in importance as remittances have provided a means of economic autonomy, but the extended
family within the 'āiga remains an important economic and
residential anchor.

Among the village's receiving families in 1969, 14 of
19 retained a three-generation extended family structure. Other receiving families not conforming to
this pattern were missing a generation (grandparent
or grandchild) due to their stage in the domestic cycle
rather than due to migration. The persistence of the
extended family may be associated with the large size of
these families and the fairly balanced sex ratio of the
migrants. By contrast, among the 7 nonreceiving
families, the extended family structure was absent,
with the grandparental generation either dead or residing elsewhere. Wiest's study (1973) of family
structure in a Mexican town suggests that where
remittances are both adequate and reliable, changes
in household structure are less likely to occur, while
under conditions of inadequate income, households alter
their structure. If this finding is applicable, it
may account for the absence of the grandparental
generation among some nonreceiving families who have
moved to another village where a son or daughter will
provide a more adequate old age for them.

Another difference between receiving and nonreceiving
families was their size. Receiving families ranged
from 5 to 27 individuals with an average size of over
12. Nonreceiving families were much smaller, ranging
in size from 2 to 9 with an average size of 7. These
differences may be associated with the ease of recruitment of relatives to remittance-receiving families,
but there are clearly other, more complex factors at
work. As Otterbein (1970) has shown, domestic cycles
under migratory conditions are often unpredictable, and
these patterns may be relatively temporary.

A chronicle of one 'āiga's experiences with migration
and remittances can illustrate some of the factors
leading to modification of both 'āiga and family
structure. Two decades ago, the Pe'a 'āiga of Sa'asi

79

was at its political and economic zenith. The titleholder, Pe'a, owned a store, held an important title,
and had powerful connections both inside and outside
the village. His own family included his wife
(Leanava) and three children, but his domestic
authority extended over another large family which
had moved into Sa'asi under Pe'a's auspices and was
rendering service to him. In the mid-1950s, Pe'a's
store was repossessed by an Apia-based firm, and he
died shortly thereafter; the 'āiga's position began to
change. By the early 1960s, all of Pea'a and Leanava's
children had migrated to Apia or overseas. The family
that had previously rendered service to Pe'a was now
independently wealthy due to remittances from its own
migrants. Pe'a's title had passed to another branch
of the 'āiga and had declined considerably in prestige.
The two branches of the 'āiga had been constantly
fighting each other and were engaged in a court action
over land holdings in 1969. By 1970, the dispute was
almost academic, for the only original member of Pe'a's
branch left in the village was his wife, Leanava. The
disintegration of the Pe'a 'āiga's political and economic
base is an extreme case of what can happen in a
remittance-dependent economy, but it provides some
insights into the dynamics of migration.

During the period that her natural children were migrating,
Leanava's adopted daughter, Misa, and her husband and
children moved in to help the aging Leanava and to
work the family lands. In 1967, the family unit con-
sisted of five members besides Leanava: the parents
(Misa and Mosamoa), who were in their late 30s, two
daughters (Fale and Eseta), ages 19 and 15, and a son
(Tavete), age 11. Mosamoa had moved to his wife's
village following their marriage and had begun
rendering service and working the lands of the titleholder to whom Pe'a's property now belonged. Because
the title had passed to another branch of the 'āiga on
Pe'a's death, Mosamoa and his family were left outside
the circles of 'āiga and village power. The low status
of Mosamoa's family within the 'āiga was similar to
that of many Samoan villagers, and, had it not been
for the involvement of Leanava's natural children in
migration, it might have remained that way.

By the early 1960s, all three of Leanava's children
had moved away from the village. The oldest daughter
moved to New Zealand with her part-Samoan husband.
The second daughter became a nurse in Apia and then
married an American and moved to the United States.

80

The son, Pula, received a good education, became a teacher, and then moved to Apia to take a civil-service post. The mobility of this family was unprecedented in the village and was sometimes resented, but the remittances sent and brought back by her children put a cement floor and metal roof on Leanava's house and paid for her several trips to New Zealand and the United States. These examples of mobility were not lost to Mosamoa and Misa, although they themselves were poorly educated and were locked into the village economic situation.

The first decision by the family was to send Fale, the 19-year-old daughter, to New Zealand. She would earn enough money to help bring the rest of the family over. Fale's fare was paid by relatives in New Zealand where she stayed with another of Misa's relatives. On arriving in Auckland, Fale almost immediately began remitting small money orders and saving for the fares. A year later, in 1968, Mosamoa was able to arrange for a work permit for himself in New Zealand and, with Fale paying the fare, he went to live with relatives for his stay of several months. He returned early in 1969 with $WS 700 in savings, which was largely redistributed to relatives in the usual Samoan fashion. If he had not done this, he would have been regarded as "the poorest of men," according to Pula who helped Mosamoa spend the money. Pula's civil service post made him instrumental in arranging Fale's and Mosamoa's immigration papers.

It was then decided that the whole family would try to obtain permanent residency in New Zealand. Fale, still in Auckland, began saving money again for fares that would total almost $WS 350 plus money to be used for other migration expenses. By December of 1969, all of the complex arrangements had been made, but a family quarrel had broken out. Leanava accused Pula, her own son, of having moved too slowly in arranging the papers for Mosamoa, Misa, Eseta, and Tavete. Other members of the family accused Pula of hoarding remittances and not sharing them with the rest of the family. Pula was crushed, because he had been working on the family's behalf, even trying to recruit labor to replace Mosamoa in the village. (With Mosamoa and his family gone, there would be no one to take care of Leanava except her adopted grandson.) Pula had also arranged for a very unusual adoption procedure to allow Eseta, Misa's adopted daughter, to migrate with the rest of the family. While tempers flared, the family prepared to depart.

Following a farewell party in Sa'asi, Mosamoa's family
came to stay with Pula in town for two days before
leaving. Although the fares had been paid by Fale,
there were still some minor family expenses that were
paid for by Pula. During this period, Pula spent $WS 3
on food, $WS 50 on clothes, $WS 5 on pocket money for
travel, and $WS 8 for the two trucks that took all the
relatives to the airport to say goodbye. As the family
raced to the airport in the middle of the night, Misa
almost decided to call the whole thing off, because
Leanava, who had encouraged migration all along, was
crying. The family took off on schedule, however, and
on December 29, 1969, Pula's sister cabled from New
Zealand that everyone had arrived safely. Mosamoa,
Misa, and Eseta would work, and Tavete would attend
school. Back in Western Samoa, relatives waited for
remittances, especially Pula, who had also just sent
his own wife to Hawaii at a cost of $WS 100 above and
beyond the fare, which had already been paid. To cover
all of these expenses, Pula had used up his salary,
$WS 50 in money orders, and a $WS 140 bank loan. The
whole experience had soured him on the idea of migration,
although he had contemplated going abroad under the
auspices of his sister. Pula felt he would rather
stay in the islands and "live like a Samoan."

In 1971, Pula himself was on the plane to New Zealand
for a seven-week work sojourn courtesy of his sister's
husband, who had found him a job in a plant. Pula
earned $NZ 78 a week and returned to Apia with a few
hundred dollars in remittances. At about the same
time, Pula's other sister and her husband in the
United States remitted a very large sum of money with
which Pula bought a new Datsun pickup truck. To take
advantage of the money-earning potential of his new
pickup truck, Pula decided to take in Sione, another
relative from Sa'asi who was at that time working in
Apia as a mechanic and trying to arrange visa papers
for migration to New Zealand. In his late twenties,
Sione operated the truck when Pula rented it out; his
job was to take care of Pula's truck and ensure that
it was not abused. From the rentals, Pula himself made
several hundred dollars between 1972 and 1973, supple-
menting his civil service and remittance incomes. He
used the money to improve his home and to pay off the
family's obligations in Sa'asi, particularly those
involving the construction of the pastor's new house.
By late 1973, Sione had finally succeeded in migrating
to Auckland. For Pula, this was a financial blow, because

Sione would be difficult to replace. However, in the
ensuing months, Sione became a regular remitter, just as
Pula and his family had hoped.

On a very small scale, this example illustrates many of
the characteristics of the wider remittance-dependent
economy: the large sums of money involved in migration,
the importance of personal networks as incentives and
as vehicles for migration, the drain of mobile individuals from the villages and from Western Samoa,
and the regrouping of social units.

TRENDS IN SA'ASI

The important trends that have taken place in Sa'asi
in relation to migration and remittances are worth
summarizing and emphasizing. Remittances have offset
losses in agricultural income and have provided Sa'asi
with a higher per capita income than other villages in
rural Western Samoa. Within the village, remittance-
receiving families have higher incomes than nonreceiving
families, producing significant wealth differences and
altering former patterns of redistribution so that the
immediate family is now favored over the wider 'āiga,
and the remittance recipient, regardless of sex or
status, is considered the legitimate agent of redistribution rather than the titleholder. Remittances
have thus weakened the authority structure and economic
unity of the 'āiga in a number of cases. Migration has
also weakened the authority of the titleholders since
it offers an alternative to village agriculture.

The income level of receiving families is dependent on
further migration and remittances. The pressures contributing to this pattern tend to perpetuate themselves
due to: (1) the generally low levels of income in the
village despite remittances; (2) the general lack of
opportunities either in village agriculture or in
village wage-labor or capital ventures; and (3) the
rising cost of living. Because the cost of imported
food and goods--the things that people buy with
remittances--continues to rise, real income is hard
pressed to match these rising costs. In addition, by
helping to fulfill family, 'āiga, and church obligations,
remittances have allowed competition within the Samoan
status system to take place for higher stakes than
would have been possible under agriculture alone.
Again, real income must increase. Because agriculture

cannot provide the necessary increments, migration and remittances continue to be a necessary part of the village economy.

While 84% of Sa'asi's population depends on remittances for about 76% of its income, agriculture, especially subsistence agriculture, remains vital to receiving families who cannot afford to completely substitute remittance income for subsistence production of food and certain goods. This continued reliance on agriculture has helped the 'āiga remain an important unit in Sa'asi even while migration and remittances have tended to erode its cohesion. Levels of cash-crop production have fluctuated over the past 15 years while migration has steadily increased. Although the agricultural decline of the 1960s helped to hasten migration, remittance dependence itself did not cause the decline nor, in the early 1970s, when migration and remittances were even more important, did it contribute to the persistence of the decline. In the early 1970s, there was a reversal and an upswing in agricultural production. This reversal, however, did not indicate a return to agriculture as opposed to migration. Rather it indicates that, even at high levels of dependence, the villagers cannot rely exclusively on remittances.

Finally, although Sa'asi has a "neoteric" quality, or quality of newness (Gonzalez 1969:10), the affluence of receiving families reflects security investments in housing, consumer goods, and church spending rather than speculative capital investment. This conservative pattern of remittance use reflects a lack of opportunities as much as it reflects conservative Samoan institutions. Indeed, the willingness of migrants and remitters to alter 'āiga patterns would tend to indicate that institutional persistence and change are related to economic, political, and social conditions rather than an inflexible commitment to tradition. While the 'aiga has been modified and those pillars of tradition-- the titleholders--have lost some of their influence, the trader and the pastor have managed to adjust more readily to remittances. In fact, these non-Samoan institutions have contributed to the persistence of migration and remittance dependence by dominating the cash-flow patterns of the villagers and, to a certain extent, determining the cash needs of the villagers.

5 Conclusions

Having presented national- and village-level data on migration and remittances, it is now appropriate to consider the broader implications of this material in light of alternative interpretations and other case material from Polynesia.

MIGRATION, REMITTANCES, AND UNDERDEVELOPMENT

The data from Western Samoa indicate that migration and remittances offer a partial *solution* to the problem of underdevelopment for families and individuals. Dependence on migration and remittances, however, is also *symptomatic* of continuing underdevelopment. Furthermore, as migration and remittances become more important at both national and local levels, they may *perpetuate* underdevelopment. That is, by more closely integrating islanders into a wider political economy, the effects of migration and remittances may prevent economic development.

This interpretation of the impact of migration and remittances is not shared by other observers of the Western Samoan economic scene. In his recent book, *Tradition and Progress in Samoa*, David Pitt contends that migration has a number of benefits. At the national level, Pitt points to the monetary and nonmonetary benefits of migration, skills acquired abroad, the employment of underemployed Samoans in New Zealand, and the "safety valve" effect of migration for young men and social misfits. He states that "migration does not usually have adverse effects on ... economic conditions generally" (1970:185) and that "overseas migration does not usually have an adverse effect on the local economy" (1970:186).

Obviously there are certain benefits for Western Samoa
at the national level, but do these benefits offset the
long-term costs of migration and remittances? Here the
evidence suggests that as migration and remittances have
become a more integral part of the Western Samoan economy,
they have helped to aggravate underdevelopment. It is
true that over the past two decades, and especially
since the 1960s, there have been dramatic increases in
the number of European-style houses, houses with metal
roofs, cars, motorcycles, and radios, as well as increased imports of luxury foods, European clothing, and
other consumer goods. These changes coupled with the
benefits cited by Pitt would seem to indicate that
modernization and economic development are taking place.
Such trends, however, cannot be considered in isolation
or as mere *additions* to the economy; they must be considered *in relation* to other trends, and in terms of
their *overall* effects, not only on economic performance,
but also on economic structure.

While consumption trends may seem to point to economic
development, there is an important distinction between
the *appearance* of modernity and the *substance* of development. The rise in consumption in Western Samoa
took place during a period when per capita income from
agriculture was falling. Remittances, as a new form of
income for part of the population, helped to offset
general losses in purchasing power and have, in part,
led to increased consumption. Yet the addition of remittances to many individual and family incomes has not
led to substantial increases in income for the population
as a whole. Real income for most of the population has
not increased markedly, even with remittances, nor have
remittances provided the capital to alter the structure
of the Western Samoan economy. Low levels of income,
despite remittances, and the lack of opportunities
have furthered migration and dependence on remittances.
Moreover, as consumption has outstripped production,
there have been serious trade and payments problems at
the national level. In 1973, the government had to
sharply restrict imports to prevent larger deficits.
It seems that remittances have helped to develop a
consumer demand well beyond Western Samoa's ability
to fulfill that demand.

Pitt does not regard the increases in consumption as a
national problem that might be contributing to underdevelopment. In fact, at one point in his book, Pitt
defines Samoan economic development as simply "levels

of Samoan consumption" (1970:15). This is a rather
unusual definition of development, since few researchers
would regard increased consumption by itself as a healthy
trend. While some *measures* of development deal exclusively with either production or consumption, *concepts*
of development usually stress increased production
relative to consumption. The inverse relationship,
increased consumption relative to production, can lead
to trade deficits and balance-of-payments problems--the
very conditions that exist in Western Samoa. The view
that Western Samoa is "only underdeveloped in a rela-
tivist sense" (Pitt 1970:2) is not supported by the
findings of this study.

At the national level, migration and remittances have
been a mixed blessing, at best. According to the Bank of
Western Samoa, by 1974 migration and remittances were
exacerbating agricultural production trends and heightening
inflation. *Pacific Islands Monthly* reported:

> The inadequate supply of taro and bananas has
> contributed to internal inflation in Western
> Samoa as supplementary foodstuffs have to be
> imported from Australia... The bank put the
> cause of lower production as the drift of many
> former small farmers and potential agricul-
> turalists to the Apia area to take up work,
> and the emigration of large numbers of Western
> Samoans to New Zealand. Remittances from New
> Zealand to families in Western Samoa fuelled
> the demand for imported food. (October 1975,
> page 79)

Ironically, in 1975, remittances to Western Samoa were
reported to have dropped by a substantial amount, and the
country was said to be in for a "bad time" until remittances from overseas recovered.

EFFECTS ON *FA'ASĀMOA*: WESTERN SAMOA AND AMERICAN SAMOA

The effects of migration and remittances on Samoan
society are, like those at the national economic level,
subject to differing interpretations. Here, too, Pitt
has found the potentially damaging effects on Samoan
custom to be negligible, commenting that "migration
does not usually have adverse effects on *fa'asāmoa*
society...." He observes:

Administrators in Samoa, relying mainly on
information from other parts of the world, have
argued that urban migration will lead eventually
to the destruction of traditional life and to
village poverty. It is argued that when the
young men migrate in sufficient numbers village
life crumbles away and the villages are left to
the old and sick who live in squalor amidst
neglected gardens waiting only for migrant remittances with which to buy tinned food
... These theories, however, have to be
considerably modified in the Samoan situation.
(1970:185)

Again Pitt cites a number of positive features of
migration and remittances: receiving families have
higher incomes than would be possible under agriculture alone, manpower losses are negligible,
migration can be used to bolster prestige, and
skills are acquired abroad. Pitt also maintains that
because migration and the use of remittances take
place within the context of Samoan custom (fa'asāmoa),
they do not undermine the basis of village life.

Some of Pitt's findings at the village level are
supported by data in this study. The villages that
Pitt studied, though, relied heavily on migrant labor
to nearby Apia and less on migration to New Zealand.
Moreover, at the time of Pitt's research in 1964, the
scale of migration to New Zealand was significantly
less than it is today; it may be that the effects of
overseas migration on a rural village without local
wage-labor opportunities are somewhat different today
than they were at the time of Pitt's research. Nevertheless, not all evidence supports the contention that
"migration does not usually have adverse effects on
fa'asāmoa society." In Sa'asi, where migration and
remittance dependence are central features of village
life, both the economic unity of the 'āiga and the
influence of the titleholders have been weakened.
Migration and remittances have not stabilized village
life, but rather have encouraged more migration and
further remittance dependence. While village life has
not been severely disrupted, and while fa'asāmoa retains
an important ideological role in village affairs, the
structure of indigenous Samoan institutions has been
noticeably undermined, although such non-Samoan institutions as the trader and the pastor have not been
adversely affected.

88

Given the amount of migration and the degree of remittance
dependence in Sa'asi, perhaps it is worth noting that
much of *fa'asāmoa* has persisted and has not been visited
by the disastrous effects that Pitt mentions. Yet there
has been a tendency by Pitt and others to place too much
emphasis on the staying power of *fa'asāmoa* while minimizing the changes that have occurred. To properly
gauge the institutional viability of *fa'asāmoa* under
conditions of heavy migration and remittance dependence,
it is necessary to compare Western Samoa with American
Samoa, where these phenomena are even more important.
Until about 25 years ago, American Samoa and Western
Samoa were in roughly the same economic situation with
an identical cultural baseline. Since then, the policy
of economic development pursued in American Samoa has led
to a very sharp difference in incomes between the two
groups of islands; in 1966, American Samoa had a per
capita income over twenty times as large as Western
Samoa (Salter 1970:22). Yet increasing income in
American Samoa has not been able to counterbalance
rising costs and lack of opportunities. Migration to
Hawaii and the U.S. mainland have taken place to such
an extent that over 60% of the population of American
Samoa now resides abroad. Ethnographer Lowell Holmes
explains:

> Samoans continue to leave the islands today
> although economic conditions have improved
> greatly. Motivations for migration include
> desire for well-paying jobs which will enable
> them to obtain material possessions beyond
> their reach in Samoa, desire for education
> for themselves or their children, and for
> some, desire to escape what they consider
> an oppressive traditional social system
> involving heavy obligations to *matai*.
> (1974:105)

Remittances are an important source of income for American
Samoans. Even in the remote Manu'a group, Holmes notes
that average remittances from overseas relatives amount
to $US 50 a month with some titleholders receiving as
much as $US 400 a month (1974:103). Such large remit-
tances have allowed the purchase of radios, television
sets, and refrigerators, as well as other prestige goods;
these feats of consumption are of a much greater magnitude
than those in Western Samoa. In many instances in
American Samoa, large remittances and/or high wages outside agriculture have led to the complete abandonment of
agriculture. Holmes describes this situation as follows:

89

While fifteen years ago every family had the
manpower to raise all of their own food, plantations now go uncultivated because family
members are off working for wages. (1974:103)

This kind of substitution of cash for agriculture has not
taken place in Western Samoa to the same degree because,
unlike American Samoa, incomes are too low to allow for
complete substitution.

Despite the apparent affluence of American Samoa, these
islands have a number of economic problems. There is
an acute trade deficit caused by consumption of imports, although this trend is not troublesome because
American Samoa's economic problems on a territorial
scale are taken care of by the United States. There is
also a continuing rise in the real cost of living and
one of the most severe areas of inflation is former
subsistence produce. Since the mid-1960s American Samoa
has been importing large quantities of the subsistence
staple taro at exorbitantly high prices. These high
prices actually opened up new opportunities for the
cash crop production of taro for export in Western Samoa
and Tonga. The acute shortages of taro were of some
concern to the government of American Samoa, and, by
1972, the U.S. Office of Economic Opportunity had spent
over $US 150,000 to encourage the planting of taro.

The attenuation of agriculture and the importance of
migration and remittances have had adverse effects on
fa'asāmoa. As in Sa'asi, patterns of authority and
redistribution within the 'āiga have been modified,
although in American Samoa, this process seems to have
gone considerably further. In a village investigated
by Maxwell (1970a), only one 'āiga in 18 observed the
traditional food-sharing pattern. Among the other 17
'āiga, gifts of food and goods were exchanged, but not
in the traditional manner. The authority of the titleholders had been eroded to the point where young men
no longer wanted to become titleholders. In the port
town area of Pago Pago, additional factors have
diminished the importance of the titleholders and even
the extended family. Village councils have lost much
of their control; in these circumstances, Holmes notes:

Violations of law tend to become police matters
rather than council matters. Pago Pago Bay area
households are extremely fluid in composition.
People come and go and rarely develop any sense

90

of belonging or loyalty. Delinquency in the
form of property destruction, truancy, pilfering,
and drunkenness has become a major problem among
teenagers. The High Court of American Samoa
now employs a juvenile officer and special
counsellors and has inaugurated new procedures
to involve the delinquent's *matai*, and thus
reinstate something of the *fa'asāmoa* influence
in the regulation of behavior of young people.
(1974:102)

In this area of American Samoa, there is a real sense of
urban poverty, the waning of communal life, dependence
on remittances and other cash income for food, and the
presence of crime. These are precisely the kind of
effects that are *not* supposed to happen to a resilient
fa'asāmoa.

It should be noted that, in at least one area of American
Samoa, the effects of migration and remittances have
been found to be beneficial to *fa'asāmoa*. In the
distant Manu'an village of Fitiuta, where 85% of the
titleholders were dependent on remittances, Holmes
found that family relationships and the prestige of
the titleholders had actually been reinforced by
migration and remittances. He remarks

the *matai* supported from abroad have high
prestige within the village. Instead of
reducing the strength of the extended family
and in turn the status of the family patri-
arch, increased mobility of family members
and increased employment of family members
in wage labor in government and industry has
strengthened his position within the village
and within the society generally. (1972:83-84)

The remittances sent to the titleholders, according to
Holmes,

strengthen the status of the extended family
and its chief by permitting greater participation in status conferring activities such
as donating generously to the church, engaging
in extravagant gift exchanges, or purchasing
prestige goods. (1974:103)

He concludes that "a good deal of modernization can take place without necessarily destroying the extended family relationship" (1972:82).

The case of the village of Fitiuta is interesting because it seems to directly contradict the interpretation of the social effects of migration and remittances presented in this study. There are some questions, however, that can be raised about this particular village and Holmes' interpretation. As noted earlier, the *'āiga* and the extended family are not necessarily coterminus, although Holmes uses the terms in this way. In Sa'asi, as the economic unity of the *'āiga* diminished, extended-family units within the *'āiga* were strengthened; perhaps a similar process is taking place in Fitiuta. Holmes also notes the strengthening of the titleholders' status as a consequence of remittances permitting generous redistribution. In Fitiuta, it is implied that titleholders have almost exclusive control over remittances and their redistribution. Nevertheless, it is possible that the titleholders' control may be due to the absence of many younger nontitleholders. In rural villages, the lack of opportunity may help to maintain the indigenous Samoan status system as long as nontitleholders continue to subsidize titleholders and as long as migrants remain away from the village. Under these conditions, titleholders can retain a measure of prestige. Should the remittances be redistributed by nontitleholders, though, the titleholders' position could be modified, as in Sa'asi. Thus, a closer look at the actual processes taking place within Fitiuta *'āiga* may yield data more in accord with the interpretation offered in this study.

It is possible that there are factors operative in Fitiuta that are not present elsewhere in the islands, but this single case is not as anomalous as it may seem. In considering the extent to which migration and remittances have had adverse social effects in Fitiuta, the more important point concerning the relationship between migration and underdevelopment may have been lost. Holmes concludes that a good deal of modernization can take place without family breakdown, but this finding might be rephrased to take note of the continuing need for migration and remittances. In Western Samoa and American Samoa, the extended family can continue to exist as a consumption unit even as its productive capacities decline. As noted earlier, however, increased consumption gives only the appearance of modernization; the general environment of underdevelopment

92

continues to encourage migration and remittance
dependence without which the look of modernity would
quickly disappear. Thus, while the particular social
effects of migration and remittances may vary, the
economic conditions leading to further migration and
remittance dependence persist.

MIGRATION AND REMITTANCES IN THE TOKELAUS AND TONGA

The effects of migration and remittances are manifest
in several Polynesian island groups other than Western
Samoa and American Samoa. The Tokelaus are one such
group where rural poverty and resource scarcity are
beginning to become evident as villages become more
tightly integrated into the wider economy. The result
is that

> some out of nearly every group of siblings
> must tāhē (emigrate) simply because the local
> resources are seen as insufficient. (Hooper
> and Huntsman 1973:404)

Land is the most critical resource in the Tokelaus and
access to it is in many ways similar to land rights in
Western Samoa. Those individuals with inadequate access
to land may either marry into a land-rich family or
migrate. The New Zealand Government has recognized
the seriousness of the problem and has helped to sponsor
Tokelau migrants. By 1969, migrant remittances outstripped income from copra production; Hooper and
Huntsman describe the now-familiar effects:

> Money has been known and used in the atolls for
> at least 100 years, but so long as it was derived
> mainly from the sale of copra produced on kāiga
> [cognatic descent group] lands it remained within
> the Traditional sphere of exchange, being dis-
> tributed, in fact, very much as coconuts are for
> food. But the money remitted by emigrants in
> New Zealand is sent to individuals, usually
> parents or other close kinsmen, and not to
> kāiga groups. Consequently, it does not enter
> into the Traditional sphere of kāiga trans-
> actions, but is spent privately on imported
> foodstuffs and other goods. Some people thus
> become less dependent on kāiga lands for their
> basic subsistence, and so less diligent about
> fulfilling their obligations to other kāiga
> members. Others become envious and dissatisfied.

93

Nuclear and extended families gain in economic,
social and emotional importance at the expense
of *kāiga*. Traditional authority patterns are
undermined. A number of individuals have built
houses of imported concrete, timber and roofing
iron, drawing on no *kāiga* resources at all for
their construction. Such houses are individual
property and not that of the *kāiga*...

Elders in the islands can no longer be considered
to be the repositories of all useful knowledge.
The authority which they hold in village affairs
is not openly questioned, but many of their collective decisions are, and elective offices are
more commonly being filled by younger men.
Similarly, the value and usefulness of collective
work are becoming less obvious, and are being
called into question also. (1973:406)

In addition, the loss of manpower has decreased leisure
time and increased subsistence inequalities. According
to Hooper and Huntsman:

There is noticeably less leisure for the men in
both Nukunonu and Fakaofo than there was in late
1967 when we began our field studies in the
islands. The late afternoon gatherings of men
for gossip and games have now almost gone, and
the flamboyant cricket competitions which gave
Tokelau life periodic excitement and *elan* lasting
a month or more over the Christmas period, are
now restricted to a few days. Some *kāiga* are
more depleted of able-bodied men than others,
giving rise to inequalities in the amounts of
foods like coconuts and fish which are available.
(1973:405)

Such trends are similar, in many instances, to trends
taking place in rural Western Samoa.

In Tonga, economic conditions are also serious. Tonga
has experienced severe hardship and has therefore had
to modify its economy quickly and drastically. Cash-
crop production has dropped, exports are down, and
prices for consumer goods are up. One correspondent
provides the following account:

Copra prices are down to 50% of the 1969 level
and nuts are occasionally bought for about 1¢
each. Many of the villages no longer contribute
bananas for export, and the sheds are locked up

except for meetings of the kava club, dances or films. Mangoes failed this year [1973], as rains washed away the blossoms. Breadfruit were late and small. Even village people are buying food from the town market. Watermelon at 20¢ to 50¢ each in 1969 now sell at $1 to $1.50. Pineapples, once 5¢, now go for 40¢ and 50¢ each. The list of high priced food is endless... But material goods are now even more widely sought, so the only answers in village minds are tourism or work overseas. (*Pacific Islands Monthly*, June 1973, page 39)

Tourism and remittances are now the two mainstays of this formerly agricultural economy. Tongans, however, have not been able to migrate as freely as they would like, and so it has been estimated that as many as 2000 Tongans have entered New Zealand illegally. In 1973 and 1974, many of these illegal migrants were deported back to Tonga.

Recently, more Tongan migrants have been allowed into New Zealand. One Tongan correspondent reports that after a six-month absence from the islands, he returned to a village that had taken on the appearance of a "ghost town" as a result of migration. More generally, services were lacking, and there was a severe labor shortage. This correspondent writes:

The Ministry of Works has had to abandon some projects because of a labour shortage and an important drainage project is grinding to a standstill for lack of workers. Over two-thirds of the carpenters on building construction have gone.

The Water Board is having difficulties because of the lack of skilled tradesmen, and the Power Board and the Government Printing Office both need more men if they are to maintain efficient operations.

Private businesses are also suffering from being short-handed . . . and what, for an agricultural country like Tonga, is worst of all, farmers complain because they cannot get enough labour to help them maintain their crops. (*Pacific Islands Monthly*, February 1975, page 35)

The economic situation has thus been compounded by
migration and it is not unusual to see prostitution
and children begging for handouts.

The effects of migration and remittances in Tonga and
the Tokelaus have taken place so quickly and so recently
that the process seems almost automatic and, to some
extent, inevitible. This, of course, is not the case,
and it is essential to consider other examples that
will illuminate the conditions that produce variability
in the pattern of migration and remittance dependence
observed in Polynesia.

THE CONDITIONS OF MIGRATION

The effects of migration and remittances are dependent
on the specific economic, political, and social conditions surrounding migration. One important set of
conditions is the degree of permanency and security
the migrants find overseas. The cases from Polynesia
presented thus far have involved mostly permanent migrants
either to New Zealand or the United States. Polynesian
migrants do not return, except for visitations, once
they are overseas and have attained a degree of security.
This Polynesian pattern, however, has important variations. Under conditions of temporary migration where
there is little security and/or where there are opportunities in rural areas, the effects of migration are
somewhat different. These variations can be illustrated
by three cases--the Siane of New Guinea, the Tonga of
Lake Nyasa, and the people of Rum Bay, British Virgin
Islands.

The Siane of the Central Highlands of New Guinea are
interesting because Siane males migrate to the coastal
town of Port Moresby in order to gain more security
for themselves when they return to the Highlands; that
is, the Siane engage in an urban-oriented strategy of
migration because they wish to pursue a rural-oriented
strategy of remittance investment (Salisbury and
Salisbury 1972). In Port Moresby, Siane males can
earn more money than they can in the Highlands, but
opportunities for investment do not exist in town, and
so remittances are taken back to the Highlands to be
used to expand coffee plantations and provide a means
of attaining prestige. The Salisbury's detailed
analysis reveals the delicate balance between different
types of opportunities in rural areas, types of employment in town, and rates of rural investment. In contrast

96

to most of the cases reviewed in this study, the Siane migrants can actually pursue speculative capital investment rather than investment in consumer goods due to the rather unusual set of rural opportunities open to them.

The Tonga of Lake Nyasa do not have the opportunities available to the Siane. The Tonga engage in a more familiar pattern of migratory wage labor where the migrant is caught between town and rural area. Van Velsen (1966) found that this pattern of migration was a result of the fact that Tongan migrants could not make sufficient sums of money to support their families in town. Low wages required Tongan males to leave their families behind with rural in-laws. The migrants then remit to support their families and in-laws and to hedge against the instabilities of urban employment. These factors provide a powerful incentive to remit; Van Velsen remarks:

> The labour migrant sees his contributions of cash and goods to the rural economy as a kind of insurance premium: "How can we expect our *abali* (kin, friends) to help us later when we are old, if we do not help them now?" (1966:163)

The specific set of conditions constraining Tongan migrants has led to a certain "continuity" in Tongan rural life.

The people of Rum Bay in the British Virgin Islands are also involved in migratory wage labor. Due to the unstable nature of employment in Great Britian, the migrants must maintain access to land back in the islands. There are, however, ambiguous claims to land, and the unrelenting pressure on land requires migrants to take special care in obliging relatives in order to insure that access is maintained. Furthermore, because there is never enough money in the islands, relatives can pressure the migrant in Great Britain to send money rather than simply relying on his good will. If the migrant fails to send adequate remittances, relatives will retaliate in an unmerciful fashion, denying the migrant access to land and ostracizing him. In his perceptive study, Robert Dirks states that "remittances are extracted from Rum Bay's migrants by coercion. In effect, Rum Bay procures remittances through fear." (1972:8)

97

These cases indicate some of the possible variations in
patterns of migration and remittance expenditure. Given
the specific set of conditions under which migration
occurs, it should be possible to predict the effects
of migration and remittances. Of course, this assumes
the existence of a calculus of opportunity employed on
both a short-term and long-term basis by migrants and
remittance recipients alike. The evidence presented
from numerous cases in this study suggests that such
an assumption is not unreasonable. Other studies of
economic processes use this assumption either implicitly
or explicitly, and a number of anthropologists have sug-
gested that the existence of "economic man" or "socio-
economic man" should be a working part of any economic
study in underdeveloped areas (see LeClair and Schneider
1968; Cook 1966; Ortiz 1967; Epstein 1975). Our study
of Western Samoan migration has relied on this assumption.
It may seem surprising, then, to find that this assumption remains a controversial one in Samoan economic
studies, and it is to this issue that the final section
of this study addresses itself.

ECONOMIC BEHAVIOR AND CULTURAL CONSERVATISM IN SAMOA

The conventional model of economic behavior assumes the
ability of individuals to maximize under a variety of
conditions. It is the variability of conditions, or
the structure of the situation, rather than differences
in ability to maximize, that are thought to produce
different outcomes. In non-Western societies, cultural
or institutional variables must be added to the model,
but these do not alter the ability of individuals to
maximize. As Belshaw observes:

> the characterization of primitive and peasant
> economies as being uninterested in maximization
> is demonstrably false... If there is a dis-
> tinction, it is because maximization is of
> different things, with different values, and
> using different methods. (1965:96)

Cultural and institutional arrangements are not invariant,
though, and within the "traditional" system of rewards
and constraints, individuals will attempt to improve
their position in a rational manner. Firth states that

> in the microeconomic sphere peasants are well
> aware of the possibilities of rational economic
> action and make strong endeavors to better their

98

economic position. In their own traditional
economy they watch margins most carefully and
switch their productive efforts accordingly.
(1969:35)

The model used by Firth and others is applicable not
only to "traditional" economies but also to changing
economies in underdeveloped areas.

As commonplace as this model may be, it does not
conform to the model of economic behavior in Samoa
presented in recent monographs by Pitt (1970) and
Lockwood (1971). These authors have pointed to the
fundamentally conservative nature of Samoan culture,
the continuity between past and present institutional
structures, and the people's satisfaction with *fa'asāmoa*.
They assign causal priority to Samoan culture and institutions, while minimizing the importance of other
forces and maximizing motivation. Pitt, for example,
maintains:

> The significant impetus for any movement of goods
> or services comes from the Samoan rather than
> the European sector... The real dynamic is an
> intense desire for European goods; the desire
> is partly explicable in traditional terms, and
> is achieved through production incentives de-
> pending on essentially *fa'asāmoa* patterns of
> reward in terms of status or goods. (1970:8-9)

While this idea is a refreshing challenge to the
conventional wisdom about the nature of economic
incentives and constraints in the islands, it is
difficult to understand how the dynamics of complex
intersocietal relationships can be understood
essentially in terms of Samoan culture and institutions.

Specifically, the model of Samoan economic behavior
offered by Pitt and Lockwood does not seem to be able
to account for adaptation to new economic circumstances
such as migration. Indeed, it is difficult to understand why migration should take place at all, given the
weight Pitt and Lockwood place on Samoan contentment
and satisfaction in the islands. Pitt finds:

> The Samoan...has his own idea of proper
> consumption and in most cases is reasonably
> satisfied with his standard of living and very
> satisfied with his way of life. (1970:266)

99

Lockwood, in his otherwise fine book, *Samoan Village Economy*, agrees:

> All the evidence presented so far points in one
> direction: Samoans are generally content with
> the life they lead. They have little interest
> in the outside world... They likewise have
> little evident concern for the future, little
> interest in productive investment, little
> willingness to 'develop.' (1971:206)

Yet if it is true that Samoans are satisfied with their
way of life and have little interest in the outside
world, why have so many Samoans left the islands and
so few returned? Pitt contends that "*fa'asāmoa* provides
the main incentive and social framework for migration"
(1970:185), but this still leaves a number of questions
unanswered. Can *fa'asāmoa* really explain the differential rates of migration from Western Samoa and
American Samoa? Why should people have to leave the
islands to participate in *fa'asāmoa*? Are wider economic,
political, and social forces of such little consequence
that they have minimal bearing on overseas migration?

The answers to these questions are not likely to be
found in the reification of *fa'asāmoa*. Without
questioning the importance of *fa'asāmoa* rewards and
constraints, it is possible to view other forces as
having an equally important bearing on Samoan economic
behavior. In terms of migration, it seems clear that
the differential income and opportunity gap between
Western Samoa and New Zealand is of major significance
in explaining Samoan migration. The number and type of
migrant visas offered by the New Zealand Government is
also an important factor in explaining the pattern of
Western Samoan migration. While these things may seem
obvious, they do need to be acknowledged.

What seems to have happened in Samoan economic studies
is that Samoans have been separated, for analytic
purposes, from their wider milieu, and subsequently
they have come to be viewed as a distinct economic and
cultural entity. In fact, Pitt and Lockwood reinforce
the distinctiveness of the Samoans by creating a Samoan
or subsistence *sector* and contrasting it to another
sector--the European or market sector. For certain
types of analysis, this kind of separation makes a
good deal of sense, and the remarks made here in no
way detract from the ethnographic contribution of

Pitt and Lockwood. Nevertheless, the dichotomous
nature of the "two-sector" approach they employ assumes
only limited interaction between Samoans and their
wider society. The economic, political, and social
forces that may have contributed to the origin, persistence, and change in the relationship between the
two "sectors" are thus reduced in significance. Rather
than emphasizing the separation and nonintegration of
fa'asāmoa with the wider world and then attempting to
assert the causal priority of *fa'asāmoa*, it might be
worthwhile to consider the factors (international,
national, and local) that have led to the changing
relationship between the two sectors.

The importance of Samoan culture and institutions has
been overstressed. It is doubtful whether any institutional or cultural complex can, by itself, act as an
economic barrier or an economic stimulus (Firth 1969:
36), and so it is necessary to move beyond *fa'asāmoa* in
terms of analysis. *Fa'asāmoa* itself cannot explain
the formation of new patterns of Samoan life during the
European colonial interlude, the existence of pivotal
non-Samoan institutions such as the trader and the
pastor, the opening of wage-labor opportunities overseas,
or the cash economy now dependent on remittances. A
monolithic, ahistorical conception of *fa'asāmoa* can
only detract from the analysis of these phenomena.

As Samoan culture and institutions are placed in a
broader historical and comparative perspective, there
will be a corresponding change in the homogenous view
of Samoan economic motivation. Samoan values such as
satisfaction and contentment with island life have
tended to be depicted in a unidimensional manner. This
sometimes arbitrary characterization of Samoan motivation may stem from the inference of Samoan psychological
and cultural predispositions without independent psychological research and without a careful consideration of
conflicting economic data. It is thus possible to read,
in the same work, that Samoans leave the islands based
on their appraisal of relative economic opportunity but
that these same Samoans do not apply this kind of
reasoning to their lives in the islands. Clearly there
is a need for more consistency as well as a need to be
aware of the variability in Samoan attitudes, which may
be considerable.

Because Samoan economic behavior often does not appear
to conform to the maximization model, it is readily
attributed to more idiosyncratic modes of explanation

101

(see Seligson 1972). Stanner (1953), however, in his
excellent but neglected work, has reminded us that the
alleged capriciousness of Samoan behavior must, in
each instance, be carefully examined before the causes
of behavior are ascribed. One instance that seems
worth reanalyzing is Lockwood's discussion of the low
Samoan labor input in agriculture; Lockwood believes
that this low input demonstrates the lack of Samoan
interest in earning money. Yet what of the long and
sometimes exhausting hours that Samoans willingly work
in New Zealand, presumably because of the money they
can earn? As for the Samoans alleged satisfaction
with things as they are, once again the statistics on
migration do not seem to follow predictions made from
such a characterization. Rather, these statistics seem
to indicate a very real concern on the part of Samoans
about their future and a sound appraisal of the results
of their own efforts in an underdeveloped economy.

A second example of the alleged uniqueness or
noneconomic nature of Samoan economic behavior involves
the use of remittances for security investments rather
than for speculative capital investments. There is,
however, nothing peculiarly Samoan about this pattern
of investment. J. L. Watson has noted the same pattern
of remittance expenditure in Hong Kong as well as in
other areas of the world, including Caribbean, Lebanese,
African, and Russian societies (1975:217-18). In
Hong Kong, Watson found remittances being used to
build elaborate houses. While he remarks that "it is
sometimes difficult to understand why the emigrants
sink their hard-earned money into non-productive
sterling houses" (1975:164), he goes on to show that
for these emigrants there are no other productive investment alternatives and that, while these houses may
not be profitable in terms of capital gain, "they are
the only investments available in a village with a
nonproductive economy" (1975:165). The lack of local
opportunities described by Watson is very similar to
the situation in the islands.

A final example involving the alleged noneconomic nature
of Samoan behavior concerns the recruitment of Samoans
for plantation labor--a problem that has puzzled
observers for some time. In the late nineteenth and
twentieth centuries, European plantations in Western
Samoa had a difficult time obtaining Samoan labor,
despite the low incomes of Samoans. This difficulty
was often attributed to the Samoans' lack of interest

in money, their resistance to sensible elements of
Western culture, and to their hopeless entanglement in
fa'asāmoa. However, a closer examination reveals that
the crucial conditions for labor recruitment lay not
in Samoan culture or in the European economy, but
rather in the economic interplay between the two (see
Gilson 1970 and Lewthwaite 1962). Both Samoans and
European planters clearly recognized the market value
of Samoan labor. In a debate involving the use of
of Chinese coolie labor in Western Samoa before the New
Zealand Parliament in 1920, the European planters
laid great stress on

> the fact that with the present price of
> copra, a native and his wife can (if they
> are in want of money) by cutting 400 lb. of
> dry copra--an easy task--earn in one day more
> than the planters could afford to pay them in
> an entire month. (in Campbell 1923:218)

As labor conditions changed, there was less trouble in
recruiting, and by the 1950s, labor demands on plantations were readily met.

All of these examples indicate that no departure is
required from the conventional model of economic
behavior to explain the economic response of Samoans;
the specification of conditions and the assumption of
rationality on the part of Samoans seems to be adequate
for explaining a variety of economic phenomena in
Western Samoa. The difference between this study and
other Samoan economic studies is that the focus has
shifted away from the Samoans themselves to the kinds
of relations between Samoans and the wider economic,
political, and social context of which Samoans are a
part. For Samoans, this wider context may become particularly critical in the near future. In the New
Zealand elections of 1975, a new government was swept
into power on a platform that pledged to sharply
restrict migration from the Pacific islands. Whether
this platform will actually become policy and to what
extent this policy will affect Samoans remains to be
seen. For the Western Samoans, New Zealand is the only
area that provides jobs in appreciable numbers, while
the remittances sent or brought back are critical to
Western Samoan economy. Since the Western Samoans are
well aware of the importance of continued migration and
remittances for their well-being, any attempt to restrict migration will be met with resistance.

103

Whatever the outcome of the Western Samoan case,
migration and remittances can only become more important for other underdeveloped areas as time goes
on. In the decade between 1970 and 1980, it has been
estimated that 400 million people are likely to migrate
from rural to urban areas in underdeveloped regions of
the world. The role of these migrants and the remittances that they bring or send back will undoubtedly
be a subject of interest to those concerned with the
causes and consequences of underdevelopment in today's
world.

Appendix:
Fieldwork and Data Quality

This appendix will provide a brief review of the fieldwork situation and a discussion of some of the methodological problems encountered in obtaining the data and evaluating its accuracy.

ORIENTATION AND FIELDWORK

Although the general perspective for the study of underdevelopment in Western Samoa was conceived before fieldwork began, the actual focus on remittances was not established until shortly after I arrived in the islands. Originally, a comparative study of village economics with substantial ethnographic emphasis was proposed, but, on arriving in Western Samoa, in October 1969, I discovered four dissertations covering precisely my proposed area of research (Fairbairn 1963; Pitt 1966; Lockwood 1968; Bryant 1966; two of these have since been published, see Pitt 1970 and Lockwood 1971). Rather than duplicating a corpus of already existing work, I decided that, by focusing on remittances, an additional dimension could be added to a body of research covering almost the entire range of topics on Western Samoa and its economy: general economic and political history, national income, agricultural history, regional agriculture, economic ethnography, population, and economic development.

My initial awareness of remittances came while living with a Samoan family in southern California between July and October of 1969. During this period, I was learning Samoan, researching the Western Samoan economy, constructing econometric models of agricultural production in Western Samoa, and, through my hosts, getting

105

a feel for Samoan village economics. From our
conversations, it became apparent that, in their
village, remittances played a significant role in local
economic life. It also seemed that the islands as a
whole were becoming remittance dependent to a degree
not fully appreciated. Thus when it was discovered
that intensive studies of village economies had already
been carried out, it seemed that the next logical step
would be to study one aspect of the economy in depth,
and my interest in remittances led in that direction.

In gathering data for this study, most of my time was
spent in the port town of Apia, where most remittance
recipients live; at the post office, where money orders
arrive and are cashed; at my relatives' house in town,
talking to migrants and remittance recipients; and at
government offices, discussing remittances with officials.
The village material is not based on long-term intensive
fieldwork in Sa'asi itself, partly due to the nature of
the subject matter. Normally, the anthropologist would
live in a village and act as a participant observer to
the extent possible, given his or her interests. Yet
with migration and remittances, the investigator must
necessarily move beyond the village if the process of
migration and the impact of remittances are to be understood. The village is only one location in which
migrants and remittance recipients could be observed.
On a practical level, villagers away from Sa'asi were
able to discuss their economic situation more openly
than they were in the village.

My actual living quarters were in town, apart from my
family, for the period between late October 1969 and
March 1970. I had visited Western Samoa in September
1966 and had been informally adopted into a family with
whom I had lived both in town and in the village. These
kin ties were maintained during the interim period, and
hence the problem of acquiring a family and adapting to
a new culture were minimized. This family experience
and the time spent with a Samoan family in southern
California led me to believe that if a problem was
selected that did not require intensive participation
or socialization, an extra-familial approach would not
adversely affect the quality of the research. In Western
Samoa, living with a family can be both an asset and a
liability. Families are often engaged in protracted
squabbles within and between themselves, sometimes en-
meshing the unwary anthropologist. There is also the
problem of the relative wealth of the anthropologist
and the poverty of the Samoans; in this situation,

106

families may compete for the researcher's attention and favors. Occasionally, this can lead members to over-protect "their anthropologist." After witnessing the debilitating effects of such overprotection on another researcher in Western Samoa, my doubts about the decision to live apart from my family were dispelled.

It should be noted that while families can be a burden on the anthropologist, the anthropologist can be a major burden on Samoan families. Although I visited my family almost daily and lived with the family in the village, they showed extraordinary patience and consideration, helping me with my research and providing good company. Sometimes I failed to appreciate the lengths to which they went on my behalf, and there is no way to repay their courtesy and hospitality.

Many of the difficulties encountered when doing fieldwork among Samoans are described in Maxwell's excellent auto-biographical article (1970b). One difficulty that he and Holmes (1974) discuss is their lack of prestige in the status-oriented Samoan social system. I also en-countered this problem, for, while relatively wealthy and American, I was still young, single, untitled, and without the powerful connections that would have offered some prestige and made research a bit easier. My lack of prestige was a problem with government officials and Samoans alike, although with Samoans the problem could be partially resolved by the use of a relative as a prestigious *tulāfale* or "talking chief," who would act as interpreter when carrying on interviews or conver-sations. The use of a *tulāfale* in certain circumstances was especially helpful, for it not only provided some measure of prestige in the formal Samoan social system, but also enabled, through translation, the avoidance of possibly touchy subjects without offending people. It also made possible interviews that I could not have carried out by myself since I was not conversant in Samoan. There was little language problem in town, where a combination of English and Samoan would suffice, but in the village, a *tulāfale* was a great help.

DATA GATHERING AND DATA QUALITY

The actual research was dictated by need for certain kinds of data, the availability of the data, and my ability to gain access to it. Basically, three kinds of data were needed: general-income data, population

and migration data, and remittance data. I tried to
gather these kinds of data on four different levels--
national, regional, village, and family--each requiring
the use of different techniques. This approach would
yield an understanding of the overall remittance
situation, while individual interviews with people at
different nodes of the system would provide insight
into the impact of remittances. Fortunately, I was
able to gather most of the data needed, and to assess
firsthand the quality of the data. For example, the
Department of Statistics allowed me to work with raw
migration data for two days in order to appreciate the
difficulties they faced in gathering reliable migration
figures at the national level. Other sources for this
material were the Department of Economic Development
and the New Zealand High Commissioner's Office, whose
officials also explained the difficulties to me. In
fact, it was not until the 1971 Census results were re-
leased that the national trends in migration actually
could be assessed, although at the village level, migration could be easily and accurately obtained through
interviews.

Remittance data were obtainable with differing degrees of
quality and accuracy. Some of the difficulties at the
national level are described in Chapter 3. To gain
some comparative insight into the reliability of remittance data on the national level, two trips of one week
each were made to Tonga in December of 1969 and February
of 1970. Tonga was ideal in terms of access and, since
I knew what to look for, prospects seemed promising.
With the aid of two Tongan research assistants, I was
able to examine migration statistics, money orders, and
general reports, and to conduct a series of interviews.
Regrettably, as helpful as the Tongan Government was,
the information did not really compare with the overall
quality of national-level remittance data obtained in
Western Samoa. American Samoa offered another possibility to examine national-level remittance figures,
but its accounting system precluded research. In spite
of some drawbacks, the national-level data on remittances
from Western Samoa were fairly accessible in comparative
perspective. The major drawback was that some kinds of
remittances were not carefully monitored. Therefore,
estimates had to be based on official reports and pro-
jections made from closely monitored remittances such
as money orders. Because money orders were available
and accessible, and because their distribution could
be mapped, a good deal of time (one and one-half months)
was spent doing exactly that.

108

From the mapping of more than 21,000 money orders
received in 1969, it was possible to gain some knowledge
of the general distribution of remittances. While
mapping, nine sample villages were selected, and their
total money order receipts for 1969 were calculated.
For one of these villages, money-order receipts were
recorded for each family. These records were then
used to check the accuracy of the family's own estimates.
Cross-checks of this sort are important, because economic
data gathered through the usual anthropological means
cannot be assumed to be accurate. There are any number
of possible sources of error, including informant hos-
tility toward economic inquiry and the fraility of human
memory. W.B. Rodgers (personal communication) has found
that in the Caribbean, there can be very large errors
in reporting the simple presence or absence of remittances without even considering the amount. In J.L.
Watson's fine study of Chinese remitters, the author
remarks that remittance income "proved difficult to
probe" (1975:135). Ember (1964:96) notes that in
American Samoa, it is extremely difficult to accurately
assess local income. Therefore, it seems that without
cross-checks on reliability, income data might well be
inaccurate.

To illustrate the problem of reliability, let us look
at money-order estimates for the village of Sa'asi.
In 1969, Sa'asi received 98 money orders, totaling
$WS 2707 in value. The total estimated by the 14 re-
cipient families themselves was $WS 2763, *an error of
less than 2%*. However, the remarkable overall accuracy
of the recipients is actually a byproduct of considerable errors by individual families. Table 15
presents family errors in money-order estimation by
magnitude and in relation to actual money-order income.
This table indicates that the chance of error exceeding
$WS 100 is almost 50% and that those families receiving
the largest sums were most likely to underestimate their
incomes by the greatest amount. Such errors were taken
into consideration when assessing the value of other
forms of remittance income.

Cross-checks were also attempted when assessing the
value of agricultural income. For agricultural income,
estimates were made on the basis of estimated family
incomes by the families themselves and data from the
trader. Some care had to be applied here, for family
income estimates were often skewed by credit involve-
ments with the trader. In one instance, villagers were
asked about the prices they were paid for their major

109

TABLE 15:

FAMILY ERRORS IN MONEY ORDER ESTIMATION
SA'ASI VILLAGE, 1969 (in $WS)

Magnitude of error	Actual money-order income	Estimated money-order income
+224.	126.	350.
+178.	104.	282.
+157.	193.	350.
+ 96.	44.	140.
+ 14.	48.	62.
+ 5.	275.	280.
+ 5.	185.	190.
+ 4.	16.	20.
- 8.	268.	260.
- 10.	110.	100.
- 15.	163.	145.
-169.	329.	160.
-176.	476.	300.
-246.	370.	124.
	2707.	2763.

Total Error = +56.

cash crop--copra. Since copra was the chief source of income for the villagers other than remittances, and since the prices were supposedly public knowledge, it was surprising to elicit some wildly inaccurate responses as well as a number of responses from people who said they did not know. A closer look at the village economy revealed that these responses were largely a product of the trader's monopoly on credit. Much of the copra sold to the trader was produced simply to maintain credit at the store, and so long as credit was kept open, people were not overly concerned about the exact amount credited to their account. Other factors leading to these responses were the fragmentary nature of copra-production process, low literacy, and absence of records. Yet Samoans were not so oblivious to copra prices that they were reluctant to take their copra to market in Apia. When they had more copra than they needed for village credit, they became more concerned with prices and took advantage of the higher prices paid in town.

The trader's income also required cross-checking and was most difficult to estimate. The estimate had to take into consideration a combination of factors-- profits derived from processing copra bought from villagers, profits from processing his own copra, profits on the sale of goods less credit, and some illegal activities that netted money. There was an additional problem in computing the trader's income as part of village income, because much of his income came from the villagers. The trader himself was quite modest, estimating that he made about $WS 60 a month or $WS 720 a year, but records at one of the firms in town indicated that the value of copra he exchanged was over $WS 4000, and this was not the only firm he did business with. Given the volume of copra that he traded and the other sources of profit that were available to him, a moderate estimate of the trader's net income for 1969 would be about $WS 1800.

This cursory examination of data sources and data reliability should lead the reader to approach the income data in this study with a good deal of care. Yet possible errors in the income data should not call into question the substantive findings on the effects of migration and remittances.

After completing research on remittances in Western Samoa, I had hoped to go to New Zealand to observe another part of the remittance network. While this visit was not

essential to the study of remittances on Western Samoa,
it would have been worthwhile in its own right. Unfortunately, I was unable to make the trip and subsequently
returned to the United States in March 1970. In May
1973, I returned to Western Samoa for a month in order
to recheck some of the data and to determine to what
extent earlier predictions were accurate.

Most researchers spend more time in the field than I
did, and their studies cover a broader area, but certain
conditions allowed me to carry out this relatively brief
problem-oriented study. I was extremely fortunate to do
fieldwork in an area with a fine backlog of supplementary
research and equally fortunate to have made the necessary
adjustments in research program and living accommodations
to begin research on remittances two weeks after arriving
in Western Samoa, and to continue almost uninterrupted
until my departure. The return trip in 1973, though
brief, was equally rewarding.

Bibliography

Abu-Lughod, J.
    1975   Comments: The End of the Age of Innocence
                in Migration Theory. *In* B. DuToit and
                H. Safa, eds. Migration and Urbanization.
                The Hague: Mouton.

Adams, R. N.
    1970   Crucifixion by Power. Austin: University
                of Texas Press.

Ala'ilima, V.J. and F.C. Ala'ilima
    1965   Samoan Values and Economic Development.
                East-West Center Review 1(3):3-18.

    1966   Consensus and Plurality in a Western Samoan
                Election Campaign. Human Organization 25:
                240-255.

Ardener, E., S. Ardener and W.A. Warmington
    1960   Plantation and Village in the Cameroons:
                Some Economic and Social Studies. London:
                Oxford University Press for the Nigerian
                Institute of Social and Economic Research.

Arrighi, G.
    1970   Labour Supplies in Historical Perspective:
                A Study of the Proletarianization of the
                African Peasantry in Rhodesia. Journal of
                Development Studies 6:197-234.

Barrett, W.
    1959   Agriculture of Western Samoa. Ph.D.
                Dissertation. University of California,
                Berkeley.

Barth, F.
   1967a   On the Study of Social Change. American
               Anthropologist 69:661-669.

   1967b   Economic Spheres in Darfur. *In* R. Firth,
               ed., Themes in Economic Anthropology.
               London: Tavistock.

Beijer, G.
   1963   Rural Migrants in an Urban Setting. The
               Hague: Martinius Nijhoff.

Belshaw, C.
   1965   Traditional Exchange and Modern Markets.
               Englewood Cliffs: Prentice-Hall.

Berg, E.
   1965   The Economics of the Migrant Labor System.
               In H. Kuper, ed., Urbanization and Migration
               in West Africa. Berkeley: University of
               California Press.

Boyd, M.
   1969a   The Record in Western Samoa to 1945. *In*
               A. Ross, ed., New Zealand's Record in the
               Pacific Islands in the Twentieth Century.
               Auckland: Longman Paul Ltd.

   1969b   The Record in Western Samoa Since 1945.
               In A. Ross, ed., New Zealand's Record in
               the Pacific Islands in the Twentieth
               Century. Auckland: Longman Paul Ltd.

   1969c   The Decolonisation of Western Samoa. *In*
               P. Munz, ed., The Feel of Truth: Essays
               in New Zealand and Pacific History. Sydney:
               A.H. and A.W. Reed.

Bryant, N.
   1966   Change in Agricultural Land Use in West
               Upolu, Samoa. M.A. Thesis. University
               of Hawaii.

Caldwell, J.C.
   1969   African Rural-Urban Migration: The Movement
               to Ghana's Towns. New York: Columbia
               University Press.

Calkins, F.
   1962   My Samoan Chief. New York: Doubleday.

114

Campbell, P.C.
    1923   Chinese Coolie Emigration to Countries
                Within the British Empire. New York:
                Negro Universities Press.

Castles, S. and G. Kosack
    1972   Immigrant Workers and Class Structure in
                Western Europe. London: Oxford Univer-
                sity Press for Institute of Race Relations.

Chen Han-sheng
    1936   Landlord and Peasant in China: A Study of
                Agrarian Crisis in South China. New York:
                International Publishers.

Chen Ta
    1940   Emigrant Communities in South China.
                New York: Institute of Pacific Relations.

Cook, S.
    1966   The Obsolete "Anti-Market" Mentality: A
                Critique of the Substantive Approach to
                Economic Anthropology. American Anthro-
                pologist 68:323-345.

Dalton, G.
    1971a   Introduction. *In* G. Dalton, ed., Economic
                Development and Social Change. New York:
                Natural History Press.

    1971b   Introduction. *In* G. Dalton, ed., Studies
                in Economic Anthropology. Anthropological
                Studies No. 7. Washington, D.C.: American
                Anthropological Association.

Davidson, J.W.
    1967   Samoa mo Samoa. London: Oxford University
                Press.

    1969   Understanding Pacific History. *In* P. Munz,
                ed., The Feel of Truth: Essays in New
                Zealand and Pacific History. Sydney:
                A.H. and A.W. Reed.

Dirks, R.
    1972   Remittances for Security: Pressuring the
                Tolian Migrant. Paper Presented at the
                71st Annual Meeting of the American
                Anthropological Association.

Dorjahn, V.R.
    1965   On Some Contributions of Anthropology to
                Demography. Anthropological Quarterly
                38:132-143.

Douglass, W.A.
    1970   Peasant Emigrants: Reactors or Actors?
                In R.F. Spencer, ed., Migration and
                Anthropology. Seattle: American
                Ethnological Society.

    1971   Rural Exodus in Two Spanish Basque
                Villages: A Cultural Explanation.
                American Anthropologist 73:1100-1114.

DuToit, B.
    1975   A Decision-Making Model for the Study of
                Migration. *In* B. DuToit and H. Safa,
                eds., Migration and Urbanization.
                The Hague: Mouton.

Easterlin, R.A.
    n.d.   Does Economic Growth Improve the Human Lot?
                Some Empirical Evidence. *In* P.A. David
                and M.W. Reder, eds., Nations and House-
                holds in Economic Growth: Essays in Honor
                of Moses Abramovits. Palo Alto: Stanford
                University Press.

Edel, M.
    1969   Economic Analysis in an Anthropological
                Setting. American Anthropologist
                71:421-433.

Ember, M.
    1964   Commercialization and Political Change in
                American Samoa. *In* W. Goodenough, ed.,
                Explorations in Cultural Anthropology.
                New York: McGraw-Hill.

Epling, P.J.
    1967   Lay Perception of Kinship: A Samoan Case
                Study. Oceania 37:260-280.

Epling, P.J. and A. Eudey
    1963   Some Observations on the Samoan
                '*āigapotopoto*. Journal of the Polynesian
                Society 72:378-383.

Epstein, T.S.
1968   Capitalism, Primitive and Modern: Some
            Aspects of Tolai Economic Growth.
            East Lansing: Michigan State University
            Press.

1975   The Ideal Marriage Between the Economist's
            Macroapproach and the Social Anthropologist's
            Microapproach to Development Studies.
            Economic Development and Cultural Change
            24:29-46.

Fairbairn, I.J.
1961   Samoan Migration to New Zealand. Journal
            of the Polynesian Society 70:18-30.

1963   The National Income of Western Samoa.
            Ph.D. Dissertation. Australian National
            University.

1967   More on the Labor Potential - Some
            Evidence from Western Samoa. Economic
            Development and Cultural Change 16:97-106.

1970a   Village Economics in Western Samoa. Journal
            of the Polynesian Society 79:54-70.

1970b   The Samoan Economy: Some Recent
            Developments. Journal of Pacific History
            5:135-139.

1971a   A Survey of Local Industries in Western
            Samoa. Pacific Viewpoint 12:103-122.

1971b   Pacific Island Economies. Journal of the
            Polynesian Society 80:74-118.

Farrell, B.H. and R.G. Ward
1962   The Village and Its Agriculture. *In*
            J.W. Fox and K.B. Cumberland, eds.,
            Western Samoa: Land, Life and Agriculture
            in Tropical Polynesia. Christchurch:
            Whitcombe and Tombs, Ltd.

Feindt, W. and H.L. Browning
1972   Return Migration: Its Significance in an
            Industrial Metropolis and in an Agri-
            cultural Town in Mexico. International
            Migration Review 6:158-165.

Firth, R.
    1946   Malay Fishermen: Their Peasant Economy.
                London: Kegan Paul.

    1963a   Elements of Social Organization. Boston:
                Beacon.

    1963b   Money, Work, and Social Change in
                Indo-Pacific Economic Systems. *In*
                J. Meynard, ed., Social Change and
                Economic Development. London: UNESCO.

    1969   Social Structure and Peasant Economy: The
                Influence of Social Structure Upon Peasant
                Economics. *In* C. Wharton, Jr., ed.,
                Subsistence Agriculture and Economic
                Development. Chicago: Aldine.

Fisk, E.K.
    1962   Planning in a Primitive Economy: Special
                Problems of Papua and New Guinea. Economic
                Record 38:462-478.

Fisk, E.K. and R.T. Shand
    1969   The Early Stages of Development in a
                Primitive Economy: The Evolution from
                Subsistence to Trade and Specialization.
                In C. Wharton, Jr., ed., Subsistence
                Agriculture and Economic Development.
                Chicago: Aldine.

Foster, G.
    1970   Tzintzuntzan: Mexican Peasants in a
                Changing World. Boston: Little, Brown
                and Company.

Fox, J.W. and K.B. Cumberland, eds.
    1962   Western Samoa: Land, Life, and Agriculture
                in Tropical Polynesia. Christchurch:
                Whitcombe and Tombs, Ltd.

Freeman, D.
    1964   Some Observations on Kinship and Political
                Authority in Samoa. American Anthro-
                pologist 66:553-568.

Frucht, R.
    1966   Community and Context in a Colonial Society:
                Social and Economic Change in Nevis,
                British West Indies. Ph.D. Dissertation.
                Brandeis University.

Frucht, R.
1968   Emigration, Remittances and Social Change:
            Aspects of the Social Field of Nevis, West
            Indies. Anthropologica (n.s.) 10:193-208.

Gann, L.
1955   The Northern Rhodesian Copper Industry and
            the World of Copper 1923-1955. Rhodes-
            Livingstone Journal 18:1-18.

Geertz, C.
1963   Agricultural Involution. Berkeley:
            University of California.

Gerakas, A.
1964   Information on Economy of Western Samoa.
            Development Secretariat Public Bulletin
            No.1, Apia.

Gilson, R.P.
1970   Samoa 1830 to 1900: The Politics of a
            Multi-Cultural Community. London: Oxford
            University Press.

Gluckman, M.
1941   Economy of the Central Barotse Plain.
            Rhodes-Livingston Paper No. 7.

Gonzalez, N.L.S.
1969   Black Carib Household Structure. Seattle:
            University of Washington Press.

Gorer, G.
1935   Africa Dances: A Book about West African
            Negroes. New York: Alfred A. Knopf.

Government of Western Samoa
1966   Western Samoa's Economic Development
            Programme, 1966-1970. Apia.

1968   Western Samoa Population Census 1966. Apia.

Grattan, F.J.H.
1948   An Introduction to Samoan Custom. Apia.

Graves, N. and T. Graves
1974   Adaptive Strategies in Urban Migration. *In*
            B. Siegel *et. al.*, eds., Annual Review
            of Anthropology. Palo Alto: Annual
            Reviews, Inc.

Gugler, J.
　1968　　　Impact of Labor Migration on Society and
　　　　　　Economy in Sub-Saharan Africa. African
　　　　　　Social Research 6:463-486.

Gulliver, P.
　1955　　　Labour Migration in a Rural Economy. East
　　　　　　African Studies, East African Institute
　　　　　　for Social Research.

　1957　　　Nyakyusa Labor Migration. Rhodes-Livingstone
　　　　　　Journal 21:32-63.

　1969　　　Introduction. *In* P. Gulliver, ed.,
　　　　　　Tradition and Transition in East Africa:
　　　　　　Studies of the Tribal Element in the
　　　　　　Modern Era. Berkeley: University of
　　　　　　California Press.

Hagen, E.
　1968　　　The Economics of Development. Homewood:
　　　　　　Irwin.

Halevy, J.
　1972　　　Southern Italy: Coming Home to Chaos.
　　　　　　Nation 215(6):489-492.

Hance, W.A.
　1970　　　Population, Migration, and Urbanization in
　　　　　　Africa. New York: Columbia University
　　　　　　Press.

Hayami, Y. and V.W. Ruttan
　1971　　　Agricultural Development: An International
　　　　　　Perspective. Baltimore: Johns Hopkins.

Higgins, B.
　1968　　　Economic Development: Problems, Principles,
　　　　　　and Policies. New York: Norton.

Hirsh, S.
　1958　　　The Social Organization of an Urban Village
　　　　　　in Samoa. Journal of the Polynesian
　　　　　　Society 67:266-303.

Holmes, L.D.
　1957　　　Ta'u: Stability and Change in a Samoan
　　　　　　Village. Journal of the Polynesian Society.
　　　　　　Part I 66:301-338; Part II 66:398-435.

Holmes, L.D.
1972 The Role and Status of the Aged in Changing
   Samoa. *In* D.O. Cowgill and L.D. Holmes,
   eds., Aging and Modernization. New York:
   Appleton-Century-Crofts.

1974 Samoan Village. New York: Holt, Rinehart
   and Winston, Inc.

Hooper, A. and J. Huntsman
1973 A Demographic History of the Tokelau Islands.
   Journal of the Polynesian Society 82:366-411.

Horowitz, I.L.
1964 Three Worlds of Development: The Theory
   and Practice of International Stratifi-
   cation. New York: Oxford University Press.

Houghton, D.
1952-53 Keiskammahoek Rural Survey: A Study of
   Failure in Social Adaptation. Economic
   Development and Cultural Change 1:350-359.

Isbister, J.
1971 Urban Unemployment and Wages in a Developing
   Economy: The Case of Mexico. Economic
   Development and Cultural Change 20:24-46.

Jones, K. and A.D. Smith
1970 The Economic Impact of Commonwealth
   Immigration. London: Cambridge University
   Press.

Joy, L.
1967 One Economist's View of the Relationship
   Between Economics and Anthropology. *In*
   R. Firth, ed., Themes in Economic Anthropology. London: Tavistock.

Keesing, F.
1934 Modern Samoa. London: George Allen and
   Unwin, Ltd.

Keesing, F. and M. Keesing
1956 Elite Communication in Samoa. Stanford:
   Stanford University Press.

Kindleberger, C.
1967 Europe's Postwar Growth - The Role of Labour
   Supply. Cambridge: Harvard University
   Press.

LeClair, E., Jr. and H. Schneider
    1968   Economic Anthropology: Readings in Theory
                and Analysis. New York: Holt, Rinehart
                and Winston, Inc.

Leibenstein, H.
    1963   Economic Backwardness and Economic Growth.
                New York: Wiley.

Lelyveld, J.
    1970   Kishan Babu. *In* W. Mangin, ed., Peasants
                in Cities. Boston: Houghton Miffin Company.

Lewis, O.
    1960   Tepoztlán: Village in Mexico. New York:
                Holt, Rinehart and Winston, Inc.

Lewis, W.A.
    1955   The Theory of Economic Growth. New York:
                Harper and Row.

Lewthwaite, G.R.
    1962   Land, Life and Agriculture to Mid-Century.
                In J.W. Fox and K.B. Cumberland, eds.,
                Western Samoa: Land, Life and Agriculture
                in Tropical Polynesia. Christchurch:
                Whitcombe and Tombs, Ltd.

Lockwood, B.
    1968   A Comparative Study of Market Participation
                and Monetisation in Four Subsistence-Based
                Villages in Western Samoa. Ph.D. Disser-
                tation. Australian National University.

    1969   Produce Marketing in Polynesian Society:
                Apia, Western Samoa. *In* H. Brookfield, ed.,
                Pacific Market Places. Canberra:
                Australian National University Press.

    1971   Samoan Village Economy. London: Oxford
                University Press.

Mamdani, M.
    1972   The Myth of Population Control. New York:
                Monthly Review Press.

Manners, R.
    1965   Remittances and the Unit of Analysis in
                Anthropological Research. Southwestern
                Journal of Anthropology 21:179-195.

Maxwell, R.
    1970a   The Changing Status of Elders in a
                 Polynesian Society. Aging and Human
                 Development 1(2):137-146.

    1970b   A Comparison of Field Research in Canada
                 and Polynesia. *In* M. Freilich, ed.,
                 Marginal Natives: Anthropologists at Work.
                 New York: Harper and Row.

McArthur, N.
    1964   Contemporary Polynesian Emigration from
                 Samoa and the Cook Islands. Journal of
                 the Polynesian Society 73:336-339.

McKay, C.G.R.
    1957   An Introduction to Samoan Custom. Journal
                 of the Polynesian Society 66:36-43.

McNamara, R.S.
    1972   Development in the Developing World: The
                 Maldistribution of Income. Vital Speeches
                 of the Day 38(16):482-487.

Mead, M.
    1930   Social Organization of Manua. Bernice P.
                 Bishop Museum Bulletin No. 76. Honolulu.

Meier, G. and R.E. Baldwin
    1966   Economic Development: Theory, History,
                 Policy. New York: Wiley.

Mellor, J.W.
    1966   The Economics of Agricultural Development.
                 Ithaca: Cornell University Press.

Mercer, J.H. and P. Scott
    1958   Changing Village Agriculture in Western
                 Samoa. Geographical Journal 74(3):347-360.

Miracle, M. and S. Berry
    1970   Migrant Labor and Economic Development.
                 Oxford Economic Papers 22:86-108.

Mitchell, J.C.
    1962   Wage Labour and African Population Movements
                 in Central Africa. *In* K. Barbour and
                 R. Prothero, eds., Essays on African
                 Population. New York: Praeger Press.

Mitchell, J.C.
    1970   The Causes of Labor Migration. *In*
                 J. Middleton, ed., Black Africa: Its
                 Peoples and Their Cultures Today. London:
                 MacMillan.

Myint, H.
    1964   The Economics of the Developing Countries.
                 New York: Praeger.

    1969   The Peasant Economies of Today's
                 Underdeveloped Areas. *In* Wharton, Jr.,
                 ed., Subsistence Agriculture and Economic
                 Development. Chicago: Aldine.

Nash, M.
    1965   The Golden Road to Modernity. New York:
                 Wiley.

    1966   Primitive and Peasant Economic Systems.
                 San Francisco: Chandler.

Nayacakalou, R.R.
    1960   Land Tenure and Social Organisation in
                 Western Samoa. Journal of the Polynesian
                 Society 69:104-122.

Neumark, S.N.
    1964   Foreign Trade and Economic Development in
                 Africa: A Historical Perspective.
                 Stanford: Stanford Food Research Institute.

Ojala, E.M.
    1969   The Pattern and Potential of Asian
                 Agricultural Trade. *In* Asian Development
                 Bank Regional Seminar on Agriculture.
                 Hong Kong: Asian Development Bank.

Ortiz, S.
    1967   The Structure of Decision-Making Among
                 Indians of Columbia. *In* R. Firth, ed.,
                 Themes in Economic Anthropology. New York:
                 Tavistock.

Otterbein, K.
    1970   The Developmental Cycle of the Andros
                 Household: A Diachronic Analysis. American
                 Anthropologist 72:1412-1419.

Pacific Islands Yearbook
1968   Pacific Islands Yearbook (tenth edition).
            Sydney.

Panoff, M.
1964   L'Ancienne Organisation Cérémonielle et
            Politique des Samoa Occidentales. L'Homme
            4:63-83.

Philpott, S.
1970   The Implications of Migration for Sending
            Societies: Some Theoretical Considerations.
            In R.F. Spencer, ed., Migration and Anthro-
            pology. Washington: American Ethnological
            Society.

Pirie, P.
1964   The Geography of Population in Western
            Samoa. Ph.D. Dissertation. Australian
            National University.

Pirie, P. and W. Barrett
1962   Western Samoa: Population, Production,
            and Wealth. Pacific Viewpoint 3:63-96.

Pitt, D.
1966   Tradition and Economic Progress in Samoa:
            A Case Study of the Role of Traditional
            Institutions in Economic Development in
            Western Samoa. Ph.D. Dissertation. London
            School of Economics.

1970   Tradition and Economic Progress in Samoa:
            A Case Study of Traditional Institutions
            in Economic Development in Western Samoa.
            London: Oxford University Press.

Plotnicov, L.
1965   Going Home Again--Nigerians: The Dream Is
            Unfulfilled. Transaction 3(1):18-22.

1967   Strangers to the City: Urban Man in Jos,
            Nigeria. Pittsburgh: University of
            Pittsburgh Press.

Read, M.
1942   Migrant Labor in Africa and Its Effects on
            Tribal Life. International Labour Review
            14:605-631.

Richards, A.I.
1961   Land, Labour, and Diet in Northern Rhodesia.
London: Oxford University Press.

Rogers, E.M.
1969   Modernization Among Peasants: The Impact
of Communication. New York: Holt,
Rinehart and Winston.

Rowe, N.A.
1930   Samoa Under the Sailing Gods. London:
Putnam.

Salisbury, R.F.
1962   From Stone to Steel. Melbourne: Melbourne
University Press.

1970   Vunamami: Economic Transformation in a
Traditional Society. Berkeley, University
of California Press.

Salisbury, R. and M. Salisbury
1972   The Rural-Oriented Strategy of Urban
Migration: Siane Migrants to Port Moresby.
In T. Weaver and D. White, editors, The
Anthropology of Urban Environments. The
Society for Applied Anthropology Monograph
Series No. 11.

Salter, M.
1970   The Economy of the South Pacific. Pacific
Viewpoint 11:1-26.

Samora, J.
1971   Los Mojados: The Wetback Story. South
Bend: University of Notre Dame.

Schapera, I.
1947   Migrant Labour and Tribal Life. London:
Oxford University Press.

Schultz, T.
1964   Transforming Traditional Agriculture.
Chicago: University of Chicago Press.

Seligson, M.A.
1972   The "Dual Society" Thesis in Latin America:
A Re-examination of the Costa Rican Case.
Social Forces 51:91-98.

Shankman, P.
1972   Review of *Samoan Village Economy* by Brian
            Lockwood. American Anthropologist 74:
            1443-1444.

Skinner, E.P.
1965   Labor Migration Among the Mossi of Upper
            Volta. *In* H. Kuper, ed., Urbanization and
            Migration in West Africa. Berkeley:
            University of California Press.

Southworth, H. and B. Johnston
1967   Agricultural Development and Economic
            Growth. Ithaca: Cornell University Press.

Stace, V.D.
1956   Western Samoa - An Economic Survey. South
            Pacific Commission Technical Paper No. 91.
            Noumea.

Stanner, W.E.H.
1953   The South Seas in Transition. Sydney:
            Australasian.

Steglitz, J.E.
1969   Rural-Urban Migration, Surplus Labour, and
            the Relationship Between Urban and Rural
            Wages. East African Economic Review
            1(2):1-28.

Tidrick, G.
1966   Some Aspects of Jamaican Emigration to the
            United Kingdom 1953-1962. Social and
            Economic Studies 15:22-39.

Tiffany, S.
1974   The Land and Titles Court and the Regulation
            of Customary Title Successions and Removals
            in Western Samoa. Journal of the Polynesian
            Society 83:35-57.

1975   Giving and Receiving: Participation in
            Chiefly Redistribution Activities in Samoa.
            Ethnology 14:267-286.

Todaro, M.P.
1969   A Model of Labor Migration and Urban
            Unemployment in Less Developed Countries.
            American Economic Review 59:138-148.

Turner, E.L.B. and V.W. Turner
    1955   Money Economy Among the Mwinilunga Ndembu:
            A Study of Some Individual Cash Budgets.
            Rhodes-Livingstone Journal 18:19-30.

Valentine, C.
    1970   Social Status, Political Power, and Native
            Responses to European Influence in
            Oceania. *In* T. Harding and B. Wallace,
            eds., Cultures of the Pacific. New York:
            Free Press.

Van Velsen, J.
    1966   Labor Migration as a Positive Factor in the
            Continuity of Tonga Tribal Society. *In*
            I. Wallerstein, ed., Social Change: The
            Colonial Situation. New York: Wiley.

Wallman, S.
    1972   Conditions of Non-Development: The Case of
            Lesotho. Journal of Development Studies
            8:251-261.

Ward, A.
    1975   European Migratory Labor: A Myth of
            Development. Monthly Review 27(7):24-38.

Ward, R.G.
    1959   The Banana Industry in Western Samoa.
            Economic Geography 35:123-137.

    1967   The Consequences of Smallness in Polynesia.
            In B. Benedict, ed., Problems of Smaller
            Territories. London: Commonwealth Papers
            No. 10.

Watson, J.L.
    1974   Restaurants and Remittances: Chinese
            Emigrant Workers in London. *In* G. Foster
            and R. Kemper, eds., Anthropologists in
            Cities. Boston: Little, Brown.

    1975   Emigration and the Chinese Lineage: The
            Mans in Hong Kong and London. Berkeley:
            University of California Press.

Watson, W.
    1958   Tribal Cohesion in a Money Economy.
            Manchester: Manchester University Press.

Watters, R.R.
    1958a   Settlement in Old Samoa. New Zealand
                Geographer 14:1-18.

    1958b   Cultivation in Old Samoa. Economic
                Geography 34:338-351.

    1958c   Culture and Environment in Old Samoa. *In*
                Western Pacific: Studies of Man and
                Environment. Wellington: Victoria
                University.

West, F.J.
    1966   The Study of Colonial History. *In*
                I. Wallerstein, ed., Social Change: The
                Colonial Situation. New York: Wiley.

Wiest, R.E.
    1973   Wage Labor Migration and the Household in
                a Mexican Town. Journal of Anthropological
                Research 29(3):180-209.

Wilson, G.
    1941   An Essay on the Economics of Detribalization
                in Northern Rhodesia. Rhodes-Livingstone
                Papers No. 5.

Wilson, G. and M. Wilson
    1945   The Analysis of Social Change. London:
                Cambridge University Press.

Woddis, J.
    1962   Africa: The Roots of Revolt. New York:
                The Citadel Press.